What To Know

Before You Go ...

Pamela Kane

illustrated by Karen Kuhrt

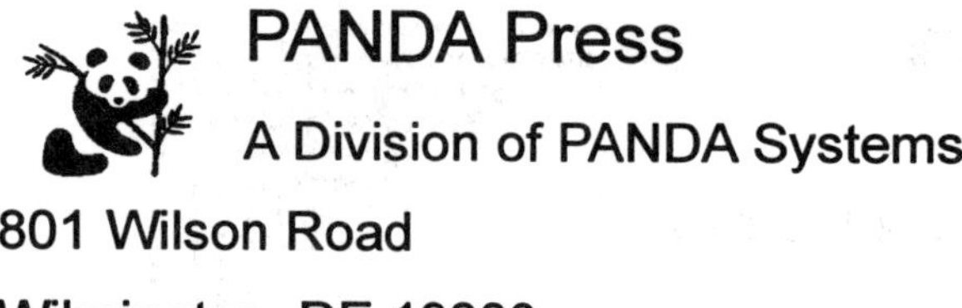
PANDA Press

A Division of PANDA Systems

801 Wilson Road

Wilmington, DE 19803

ISBN: 0-9644144-0-6

Library of Congress Catalog Number: 99-091480

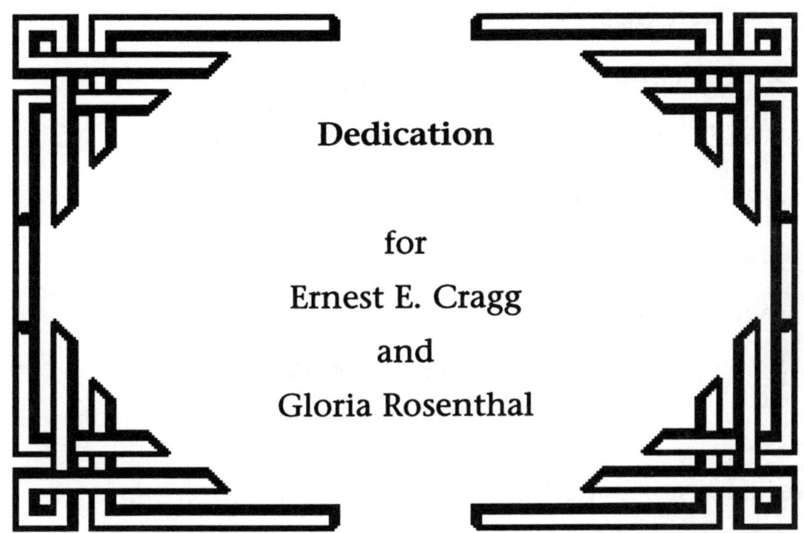

Dedication

for
Ernest E. Cragg
and
Gloria Rosenthal

and to Andy's co-worker, Ed,
and his wife, Ann.

Happy Sails!
Pam

TABLE OF CONTENTS

ACKNOWLEDGEMENTS

First, Ernie Cragg. Ernie has touched my life with inspiration, dedication, faith and good humor.

Second, Gloria Rosenthal. I knew how to spell courage; she taught me the definition.

Now, it's time to, as they say in the land of Oz (Australia), "Shout a round" for the people without whom this book wouldn't be in your hands.

Champagne for a host of people – too many to count or, even, begin to remember – from the cabin steward on our first cruise who lined up my glasses in rainbow fashion on the cabin's windowsill, to the Captains who entertained us at their tables. They are the people who make our cruises so extraordinary. One shining star – Lisa Anderson, Social Hostess on *Meridian* back in "the day."

Casting the "Net" wider, the people I've come to know on cruise and travel Internet bulletin boards. We've shared knowledge, experience and insights for a long time. Without that freedom of friendly interchange, a book like this would never have come to be. Liebfraumilch for the Floating Sisterhood of Blue Nuns, world cruisers who know the value of elastic waists, small ships and exotic ports. A special umbrella drink for Jack Adler, Captain, Chaplain, and Dance Host on the AFLOAT/Cruise areas of the PRODIGY Services. He's been my harbor pilot through rocky shoals and can never be thanked enough.

From my Internet homeport – known as "HW" – Gloria Rosenthal, David Feldman, Jim Cypher, and Tad Richards – for shared stories of the publishing wars, sound advice, and solid friendship. Peg Bowen for endless frogs and comics. Charlie Alexander as my conscience. Debbie Puente for making me remember the excitement of a new book and to want, after too long away, to do it again. Suzanne Heatherington for tolerating a two-week cruise with me. Neala Schwartzberg for creating calm out of chaos. Joanne Monkling for keeping the conversation going. Patrice Fitzgerald for legal advice and sharing my love of cruising. Myrna Courtney for Green Hungarian when I needed it. Stephanie Mathias for lots of "You Go! Girl" KINTPs. Jenn Low for providing cyber *feng-shui*. And, of course, the other two of the Terrible Troika, Nancie Meng and Claire Szopa. Triple Mobleys for everyone.

Another HW, Ruth Bavetta, deserves special mention as my careful, consistent, conscientious copy editor. Here's a nice Merlot for you, pencil-woman.

And I have to thank the nameless fellow, a travel writer whom I met while sailing the South China Sea. He told me I would never be able to break into the travel writing business. If you're out there, guy? Thanks for the challenge.

Without Bill Panoff, publisher of *PORTHOLE* Magazine, and Lesley Abravanel, *PORTHOLE's* Managing Editor, that fellow might have been right. Thanks, Bill, for the Foreword and the chance to share pages with you. Here's a nice Australian Shiraz. Some Ketel One with an albatross on the side for Lesley, bartender. Thanks, too, to Phil LaPadula who keeps the facts straight and the punctuation proper. And Ann Drew for talking shop plus having both creativity and the organizational ability to herd cats. Particular gratitude to Dale Rim who gave me a "rim shot" when I needed it. The margaritas are on me.

A case of Blue Hen beer to cover designers Ed Schmidt and Paul Thien. A champagne brunch at the legendary Green Room for Nick Cerchio of Cedar Tree Press for just being Nick – and twenty years of friendship. A bottle of *really* good champagne for illustrator, Karen Kuhrt.

Some fine single-malt Scotch for my partner in travel and in life, Andy Hopkins. And a weak VO and water for Mom. Finally, I've written a book you can understand.

INTRODUCTION

WHAT THIS BOOK ISN'T

This book won't tell you how to book a cruise, how to choose a ship or how to select an itinerary. There are big, fat books with famous names like Fodor's, Fielding's, and Berlitz to do that. It also doesn't contain time-sensitive information on ports of call. There are excellent guidebooks, particularly the Lonely Planet series, to do that.

There are also the vast resources of the Internet and, of course, your own travel agent whether in Cyberspace or in your home town to find the best cruise deal. If you have yet to choose an agent, make sure he or she is certified by CLIA, the Cruise Line Industry Association. In the best of worlds, your agent is associated with a cruise-only agency.

WHAT THIS BOOK IS

This book contains everything those big, fat books don't tell you. And, possibly, what some travel agents can't, won't or don't tell you. These everyday tips and details will put you in control of your cruise experience.

And it's not just for first-time cruisers. If you have cruised before, you know that there are things you would have done differently. In these pages, you'll learn how to do it better. Experience is, often, the best teacher. There's no need to reinvent the wheel or the sail.

GENERALLY SPEAKING ...

Throughout this book, the words "generally" and "usually" appear with great frequency. For a good reason. Even at the Millennium nobody can know everything about every cruise line and its fleet on any given day. I've drawn on my own cruise experiences and those of other cruisers who joyfully and selflessly enrich the Internet with their own experiences.

HOW THIS BOOK CAME TO BE

My husband took me on a cruise to Bermuda for our fifth wedding anniversary. I'd not wanted to cruise before; the idea didn't appeal to me. But something happened as we sailed out of New York Harbor. I was hooked. So hooked, in fact, that by our eleventh anniversary we'd visited 43 countries on six of the seven continents. On cruises. Hooked, in spades. On that first cruise, I was the novice of all novices. Now, I'm not.

Over the past few years, I've answered countless questions on the Internet and I've also written an advice column in a national cruise travel magazine. I wonder if there isn't a cruise-related question I haven't heard.

In this book, I'll try to answer them all – and add in a few of my own that you may not have thought of yet.

HOW THIS BOOK IS ORGANIZED

Simple. Front to back. We start off by thinking about packing, then we pack, and so on. We end up with the tidbits that didn't fit anywhere else.

Throughout the book you'll see Ernie, the seagull. Ernie points out extra-special tips, tricks, or traps.

Sail on.

About The Author

Pam Kane is a devoted cruiser and an internationally-known nonfiction author. Before turning her attention to travel journalism, she wrote nine books on computer-related subjects, particularly in the areas of computer security and on-line communications

In a previous incarnation, she was Senior Contributing Editor of *Portable Computing* magazine and a Contributing Editor of *HomePC* magazine. Her work has appeared in every major computer-related magazine and has been translated into eleven other languages.

She has appeared on such major television venues as the CBS Evening News, Good Morning America, and The Financial News Network. She has been interviewed by every major radio network and has been featured on both PBS' Science Friday with Ira Flatow and the Osgood Chronicles. Before her husband's retirement as a radio air personality, she frequently shared the microphone with him at his Philadelphia radio station.

Today, she is the publisher of an Internet-based magazine which covers arts and popular culture, is an editor of *Travel World International* and contributes regularly to the cruise travel magazine, *PORTHOLE.*

Home port is Wilmington, Delaware, which she describes as "The corporate capital of the world and the shoulder of the fast lane." It's close enough to the head of the Chesapeake Bay that she and Andy can trailer their yard yacht, OffLine, a 5.2 meter Boston Whaler Harpoon, to the head of the Bay for an afternoon sail when the breeze is fair.

FOREWORD

There is no such thing as the average cruiser. But every cruise enthusiast, whether a first-timer or a seasoned veteran, has questions about the Cruise Experience.

I can vouch for this, having the privilege of ten years' experience as a senior Cruise Director with Carnival Cruise Lines. Now, two decades later, as editor-in-chief of *PORTHOLE*, my passion continues to be informing, educating and entertaining current and future cruise enthusiasts worldwide.

During my years aboard ship, I learned that even though every passenger is unique, there exists a common collection of questions about cruising. Every cruise director, travel agent, or cruise industry professional has heard a variety of these questions.

Some will tell you they have heard them many times over. They are genuine, serious questions about the cruise experience; questions that need answering. But we can't answer them all in every issue of our magazine.

That's why I am delighted that Pam Kane has decided to write *CRUISE CONTROL*. Her credentials, both as a world cruiser and international best-selling author, come together seamlessly in this book. It is packed with experienced insights, common sense, and the engaging spirit of fun that make her a favorite with *PORTHOLE* Cruise Magazine readers.

The modern day cruise industry continues to enjoy phenomenal growth. In the two years before the turn of the century, the number of cruise passengers increased ten percent. In 1999, 2000, and 2001, more than 25 new cruise vessels will be launched into service.

Our extended "family" just keeps on growing.

Whether you're planning your first vacation at sea, just beginning to get your sea legs after a cruise or two, or have cruised as much as my wife and I have, this book will give you the tools you need to position yourself solidly at the helm of your own unique cruise vacation experience.

Keep cruising!

Bill Panoff
Editor-in-Chief
Porthole Cruise Magazine

Bon Voyage

Chapter One

Clothes Line

But I don't have anything to wear! Don't shout. Of course you do. Your entire closet is full of wonderful clothes and, unless one of your neighbors is going on the cruise with you, your clothes will be new to your "audience."

Don't be disturbed by the images you saw in *Titanic.* You don't have to be that dressed up for dinner every night.

In this chapter, we'll explore what a cruise wardrobe is – and isn't.

What's for Dinner?

The three wardrobe buzz words for cruising are Formal, Informal, and Casual. They are codified by the men's dress for dinner.

On a seven-day cruise, the first and last nights are always casual. On the first night, you may not have time to change out of your travel clothes; on the last night, you're packed – or almost so. On longer cruises, the mix remains much the same; there are just more nights to plan for.

Formal nights, in general, are after at-sea days and feature the Captain's Welcome and Farewell parties.

The other three nights are up for grabs, often depending on your itinerary, but count on at least one or two as Informal. The later the departure from a port, the more likely that night will be designated as Casual.

Now That We Have the Words, Let's Add the Music.

Formal means, almost, just that. And gives rise to the #1 question asked by first-time cruisers: Does my husband need a tux? In a word, no. A dark business suit, preferably worn with a white shirt and subdued tie, is perfectly acceptable. These days less than half the men seem to be tuxed-out on formal nights. If the man doesn't own one but would like to shine in the casino *a la*

James Bond, tuxes are available for rent through the cruise line. Right down to the shoes.

Three tux rentals, whether on land or sea, probably cost more than the purchase of the entire livery.

Ladies have more leeway and take it. Although a ball gown might be a bit intense unless you're taking a New Year's Eve cruise, anything you would wear to a dressy evening wedding works. Mother-of-the-Bride dresses often get a second outing by going along on a cruise. Short cocktail dresses and laid-back silk pants and jackets are always in fashion.

Interestingly, formal tends to be less so on Alaska cruises – perhaps because the ladies don't have a tan to display?

Ship's dining rooms are famous for their aggressive air conditioning, so a light sweater or other kind of shoulder warmer is important if the upstairs of your dress doesn't provide full coverage. Even in high summer – or when cruising the tropics in winter – long sleeved dresses are fine.

Informal for men usually means sports coats and ties. With pants. A collared knit shirt under the uniform blue blazer passes muster, too. The only exception to the no shorts dining room rule is made – on cruises to Bermuda – for men who appear on informal nights in "Full Trimingham" – navy blue blazer and perfectly hemmed Bermuda shorts, with the requisite knee socks which complement the color of his tie. For women, move the wedding up to the afternoon or think going-to-church-with-brunch-afterward, or any cocktail party where the significant other would wear a blue blazer or sports coat, tie or not.

Casual seems to cause the most problems. Jeans on men (or women) are not appropriate at dinner, though the rule is relaxing somewhat for well-pressed, tidy designer denims. Absolutely no T-shirts on men, though ladies can skate through with an attractive, well-fitting T if it's part of an outfit. Casual khakis and collared shirts – knit or otherwise – do the job for the males. The distaff side of the fashion equation has more latitude, but casual is not the night for silks, satins, and frou-frou dresses. The fash-

ion police won't check at the dining room door to see if you're wearing pantyhose on a Casual Night.

A subset of casual, found on upscale lines, is "Country Club Casual." Much dressier. If you can afford the cruise, you probably already have the clothes.

As a practical matter, first impressions do count and, casual first night out, you meet the people you'll be dining with for your entire cruise. (More on this in Chapter 5.) It's not the time to look like a vagrant, nor is it the time for the Ivana Trump look.

Don't worry too much about other people's opinions of your fashion statements. I only remember two women's dresses, possibly because of the women themselves. One, a horrid bright red sequined number, a bit too tight, worn by a redhead. The other, a stunning floor-length black silk column of a dress with the smallest spaghetti straps. The straps were studded with rhinestones. Just the straps. The lady must have been six feet tall.

What if we don't want to dress for dinner on a formal night?

Some people just plain don't enjoy dressing up, though the majority of cruisers do. If your ship has an alternative restaurant – and most do these days – Formal Night is the time to try it. Failing that, there's always room service.

If I do decide to buy a tux – and there are two formal nights – don't I need two formal shirts? They're expensive.

They're less expensive to launder than to purchase. I doubt there's a professional laundry anywhere on land with more experience in pleated-front shirts than any ship's laundry, accustomed to keeping its officers in perfect bib and tucker. Heresy though it may be, if you don't spill soup on your starched front or perspire too heavily at the $5 blackjack table, you can hang the shirt up for airing and give it a second wearing.

My husband is a military officer. Can he wear his full-dress uniform on formal night?

Sure. And if he is a Scot, he could wear full-dress kilts and sporran. Other formal ethnic costumes are also appropriate and add a wonderful touch to the evening.

We're taking our kids along on the next cruise. What should they wear?

Little girls are usually well-supplied with party dresses, courtesy of doting grandmothers, so formal nights should be no worry. Informal nights equal Sunday School togs; a nice school outfit will do for casual nights. Once fashion maturity sets in – usually around the age of ten – woe be unto the parents who attempt wardrobe guidance. If your teen or almost-teen has been to a dressy dance or a prom, one formal night is taken care of. Surely she has a friend who's the same size – she can borrow the pal's finery. Don't even suggest she wear the same thing twice.

Little boys are not junior men – don't ever trick out the heir to the family fortunes in a miniature tux or, for that matter, anything resembling a coat and tie until he's old enough not to look like something in a Busby Berkeley movie. Then the standard navy blazer, khakis, shirt and tie are fine for formal night – even with sneakers. The blazer reappears over a polo shirt for informal nights and stays in the cabin on casual night.

For children of both genders, the no jeans and no shorts rule applies in the dining room if the offspring is past nursery school age.

How do I know what the other women are going to wear? I don't want to look out of place.

On formal nights, you'll see everything from enough sequins to keep every matador in Spain happy, to a simple black dress with pearls. The gap widens on informal nights when the black dress with pearls is the dressier end of the continuum and a cotton sundress with sandals is the less fussy other end of the fashion line.

Casual nights are simply that. Mid-cruise casual is less casual than the first and last nights when it's expected you might be wearing your travel clothes.

You're going to over-pack anyway, so give yourself some suitcase shopping room. Take along one outfit that could work for a laid-back formal appearance or a dressy informal evening and another one – or two – which transcends informal and casual. Keep in mind that the scheduled dress code you receive with your travel documents is subject to change.

Are there any truly hideous fashion mistakes? I don't want to make one.

Some people consider over-dressing to be a mistake, but that's hard to accomplish on a cruise ship. There is plenty of competition. Good taste should rule.

In general, lose the gold and silver lamé, let the ship's officers wear the uniforms, and avoid garments featuring anchors, life rings and jeweled sea creatures.

The worst mistake is taking something that zips or buttons tightly, earmarked for a night toward the end of the cruise. Elastic waists are more than useful and desirable. They are salvation.

What about the rules for summer dress – white dinner jackets for men and white shoes for women – supposedly only between Memorial Day and Labor Day? Our cruise is in February.

There's a simple seafaring rule about white dinner jackets. If the Captain is wearing whites, it's appropriate. If not, it's not. But who pays attention to those old rules anyway? Captains often wear whites in the Caribbean in winter.

The white shoes rule is suspended when winter-cruising in the tropics.

Is it OK to change into something more comfortable after dinner?

Cruise lines are quite clear – the dress code of the evening is the dress code. However, the number of people who dart back to their cabins and exchange dress-up for dress-down may indicate that a certain portion of the passenger public is illiterate.

Excuse me? I paid for this cruise! Why can't I dress any way I want to?

With a few exceptions, you can. At your own risk, so far as the impression you make on other passengers.

Eighteen Hours – The Rest of the Day

So much attention is given to after-six attire, it's easy to forget that you do need to be clothed for the rest of the day, at least outside your cabin.

If your cabin is on a promenade deck, immediately check to make sure that your windows are, indeed, one-way glass. There are two methods to accomplish this. First, and more practical, dispatch one person to walk outside on the deck and look in. Second, stand nude in front of your window and wave at passers-by. If they wave back, you have your answer. The daytime view may be different than that after dark. Check again.

Daytime shipboard dining is much more relaxed, as is the dress code for activities that don't take place on the pool deck, but there are still a few rules. Shorts and jeans are allowed in the formal dining rooms and other public rooms, but that means dressy shorts or jeans purchased within recent memory and a nice shirt. It does not mean sweaty running shorts, cut-offs or out-at-the knees Levis and ratty T-shirts emblazoned with the name of your local biker bar. The casual buffet-type restaurants are more forgiving and merely ask for a semi-modest cover-up and dry bathing suits beneath. The bathing suit rule comes up much less frequently on Alaska and Fall Foliage itineraries, when you're much more likely to be worrying about how many layers to put on or take off.

The same clothes you wore to breakfast in the formal dining room are perfectly appropriate for port visits. Teenage girls and younger women with great figures are cautioned not to display too many feminine charms ashore, whether touring or at a beach. It's one thing to offend the locals' sensibilities, quite another to excite and, possibly, incite members of the opposite sex.

Those breakfast-type clothes come into play again in the late afternoon, if you've spent the day beside the pool or at the beach and want to spend a few hours lazing in a deck chair, going to tea, or participating in organized activities.

Plan on at least two bathing suits per person. There's little worse than struggling into a clammy suit that didn't dry overnight.

Underpinnings

There are two main schools of thought regarding ocean-bound underwear. Some people pack their oldest garments, with the intention of pitching them out along the way. These efforts are sometimes thwarted by conscientious cabin attendants. The other attitude is that it's high time to spiff up the contents of the underwear drawer with replacements. Quantity is a larger problem, especially on longer cruises. Most people simply don't have two weeks' worth of basic underwear, new or old.

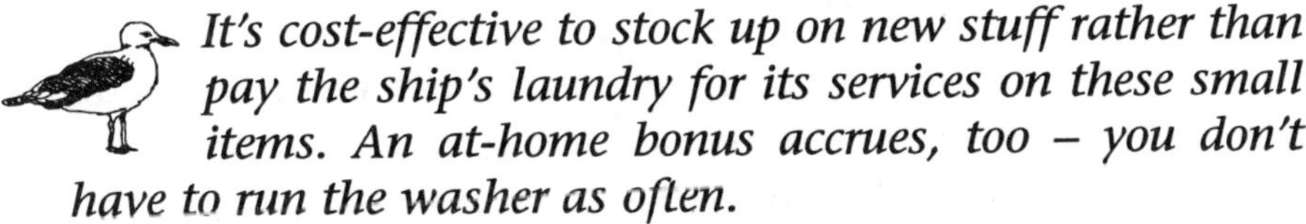

It's cost-effective to stock up on new stuff rather than pay the ship's laundry for its services on these small items. An at-home bonus accrues, too – you don't have to run the washer as often.

How many of anything you need depends on your personal comfort level. The obsessively fastidious may require three changes of undergarments a day. Ladies require not only the basics but, often, a special bra or slip for a special dress. Count out your anticipated use of foot coverings – athletic socks for both genders, dress socks for men and pantyhose for ladies. Buy more if you need them; they don't take up much space.

Nightgowns and pajamas and whether or not to wear them are strictly matters of personal preference. Remember that someone has to open the door for the relentlessly cheerful person carrying your morning coffee on his or her silver tray. Robes are altogether too bulky to consider packing unless they're a lightweight silk or cotton. Boxer shorts are sufficient to handle the modesty problem for gentlemen and are perfectly suitable for in-cabin lounging attire.

Like many luxury hotels, some cruise lines supply terrycloth robes emblazoned with the company crest, in your cabin, especially the suites. You can even take the robe with you when you leave – for a fee. Don't worry. If you forget to tell them that you took the robe, someone will notice and they will happily charge your credit card.

We're going to Alaska. How cold is it going to be and what do we need to pack to keep warm?

The Alaska cruise season runs from late May through September. Strangely, the locals call that time of year summer and tourists seem to anticipate Antarctica. But you can be cold, darned cold, especially on top of glaciers or standing on a weather deck watching calving in a bay. The earlier or later in the season you travel, the more chilly it's likely to be. Bulky parkas are a packing drag. You'll do just fine with a layering approach topped by a windproof, hooded jacket.

Take a hint from skiers of both gender persuasions: one of the warmest first layers you can put on is a pair of heavy-duty, support-type pantyhose. There's nothing gender-specific about the ideal cold-snap Alaska garb. Underwear, pantyhose, socks, turtleneck, polo shirt, sweatshirt or cotton sweater, chino-type pants or jeans (too-tight jeans provide next to no insulation value) and your windproof, rainproof jacket. A pair of gloves and a ski-type headband to cover your ears complete the ensemble.

A polo shirt over a turtleneck sounds a bit strange, but you'll be glad to have it available – especially in port – if a shivery morning turns into a sunny, warm mid-day.

If you don't pack generic shorts, the weather will be in the high '70s or low '80s. I promise.

Windsuits, the crinkly, flannel-lined nylon pants and jacket, are highly recommended for both men and women. Worn with a polo shirt or a turtleneck, they're the happy medium dress for medium weather. And if things are really frigid, they'll zip over your cold-snap uniform.

Can't I EVER wear a T-shirt on a cruise?

Of course you can. They're just not particularly appropriate in the formal dining room or other public rooms during the day and are never appropriate at night. T's make fine cover-ups for the casual buffet restaurants and can be dandy conversation starters whether you're a walking billboard for the home town, making a philosophical statement, "*Give Me Chocolate and No One Will Be Hurt*", or advertising the fact that you've visited exotic places from Singapore to Sydney or Australia to Zanzibar.

We live in the Snow Belt and are taking a Caribbean cruise in January. What do we do about our heavy coats?

In the best of all possible worlds, you'd be dropped at the airport by your driver – whether professional, family member, or gracious friend – and be picked up the same way, your coats at the ready.

Professional limo drivers will hang on to your coats for you. Tip well, in advance.

If you're driving yourself to the port or airport, you can leave the coats in the car and be prepared to shiver a bit while the car and the coats warm up. What you don't want to do is lug parkas through airports and, worse, figure out where to store them in your cabin. If all else fails, rent a locker at the airport.

10

Packing It In

Packing is an art and a craft. The primary goal, that your clothes don't look like they traveled in a lawn and leaf bag, is joined by a secondary goal, ease and speed of unpacking. My long-standing personal best for unpacking is 13 minutes flat – *Legend of the Seas*, October 1998, San Diego – for a 15-day Panama Canal cruise. In this chapter, I reveal my packing system, starting with the plans and schemes for a tropical cruise.

Some Assembly Required

In an ideal world you'd have your own "cruise closet" and a room you can dedicate solely to the exercise of getting organized pre-pack. Not everyone has that luxury. Even those of us who do can find ourselves out of luck when an adult child pops in for a weekend and ends up staying a month.

Desperate situations call for desperate measures. Cruise over to your local discount department store and purchase three of the over-door cantilevered hanging devices you'll find in the closet department. While you're there, pick up several of the hangers that hold a top, plus shorts, pants, or a skirt. The best kinds hang on each other, saving space. Don't leave yet. Score a hanging shoe bag – the kind with little shelves. And, if you don't have them in the pantry, quart-, gallon- and two gallon-sized zippered plastic bags. Then hit the electrical department for a bag of small cable ties. Don't ask, just buy.

Put those cantilevered hanging devices over one or more of the doors in your bedroom. Now your bedroom doors are your cruise closet. Once you're done ironing, the ironing board can be pressed into service for staging operations. If you have a cat or more hanging around the house, make sure the furry felines know that sleeping on the stacks of freshly washed and ironed clothes is a no-no. You can use the spritz bottle that you used to dampen clothes while ironing to discourage Tabby from taking up residence.

The Laundry Moment

This is a two-part exercise. Visit your local laundry and dry cleaning establishment with your cruise clothes unless they're already hanging, neatly, in the closet from their last visit, still in their plastic shrouds. Even if you normally do shirts and casual trousers at home, give them a treat. Ask that the shirts be folded, not hung. There's a reason for this. When you pick up your clothes, ask the counterperson for twenty more plastic bags. Offer to pay for them. There's a reason for this, too.

Two days before you are to leave, do your laundry. All of it. Having everything at hand, clean, cuts packing time dramatically. What you don't want to do is start making little stacks here and there two weeks ahead of time. You'll forget what you've stacked and mess up the stacks looking through them. Designate underwear and clothing for your pre-departure day and travel day.

Though I don't make a habit of it generally, I do iron knit shirts and T-shirts pre-cruise, as well as my husband's silk boxers. They just look and feel nicer.

Pack-Day – Phase One

Start the final staging process early in the morning of your pre-departure day. This gives you plenty of time to rush out for last-minute emergency purchases and permits the use of your unoccupied bed for stacking. For the average couple, This initial phase requires the equivalent of two 24″ suitcases and one 26″. But you may need more.

Turn on the radio, put up the over-door hangers and start hanging. First, hang dresses for formal nights. Then, locate the associated accessories – jewelry, special lingerie, shoes, evening bag. Put them on the ironing board (shoes underneath). Do the same for each additional formal, informal and casual evening outfit. Most women require two over-door hangers for this task.

On another over-door hanger, put the tux or dark suit, sports coat or blazer with associated pants, and casual pants. Now, find the studs and cufflinks, dress shoes and dress belt. Put the studs and belt on the ironing board if there's any room left and put the shoes underneath.

If any of the clothing items aren't encased in a cleaners' plastic bag, use your extras. Once in the suitcases, the plastic slides nicely on itself and the small amount of air trapped inside almost totally prevents wrinkles.

Next, men's shirts. Plop the folded shirts, in their bags, on the bed. Choose a tie and socks for each shirt and slip them inside the bag. Bow tie, cummerbund, suspenders, and proper socks go in the bag with the dinner shirt.

Stack the shirt-packs on the pillows at the head of the bed, out of the way.

Everyday clothes are next. We send my husband's shorts to the professionals so they're already on hangers and in bags, but hanging is optional. Count out men's shorts and stack neatly. Next, count out men's polo-type shirts – at least one per day – and stack next to the shorts. If he prefers short-sleeved sport shirts that you've laundered and ironed at home, they should be on hangers. Add two bathing suits, then underwear and socks according to your calculation of need. If special clothes are required for athletic endeavors, put them out now. Add a cotton sweater for chilly evenings.

A sport or polo shirt worn only to dinner or around the ship in the afternoon can be recycled the next day, saving packing space.

While men tend to think in terms of interchangeable shirts and pants, women are more outfit oriented – this shirt with those shorts, and so on. That's where your new hangers come in. Put your outfits together, whether folded or hung, and make sure any accessories land on the ironing board.

On the bed, stack your swimsuits, cover-up, bras, panties, pantyhose, slips, socks, nightgowns and in-cabin lounging apparel. I favor full-length cotton caftans – they're equally appropriate in the cabin or on deck. Don't forget a cotton sweater and a dressy sweater or shawl for evening.

If you're T-shirt kind of people, stack 'em up now. There should be enough room left at the foot of the bed for a suitcase. Look at your watch. If this entire enterprise took more than an hour, you probably took a coffee break.

Break out your zippered plastic bags. Shoes, particularly athletic shoes, should not be put next to your wardrobe. Bag the shoes, then bag your costume jewelry and other small accessories outfit-by-outfit. Your fine jewelry should travel with you at all times.

Flat-out – Phase Two

The suitcase moment has arrived. Transfer your stacks of flat-foldeds, neatly, into the waiting luggage – the two 24" pieces. If you're anywhere near normal, one suitcase will be almost full of "his" things and the other quite full with "hers". Large flat items such as ironed shorts, go best in the bottom. Add shoes and accessory bags. This is the stunning moment when you'll know if you might need another suitcase.

If the bags are full or almost full, close them and lug them to an out-of-the-way place where they will lie quietly on their sides until you're ready to leave. They'll be available for you to squeeze in one last thing, if there's room.

There's no reason not to pack the hanging items next, but some people prefer to wait until the last possible moment. Start with the men's pants, on their hangers, on the bottom. The hook of the hanger rotates over, but be careful when you turn it. Sometimes the sticky substance that keeps the pants on the hanger produces nasty wrinkles that you won't see until you unpack. After that, just keep adding garments, with the blazer and suit coat or dinner jacket on top. *Voila!*

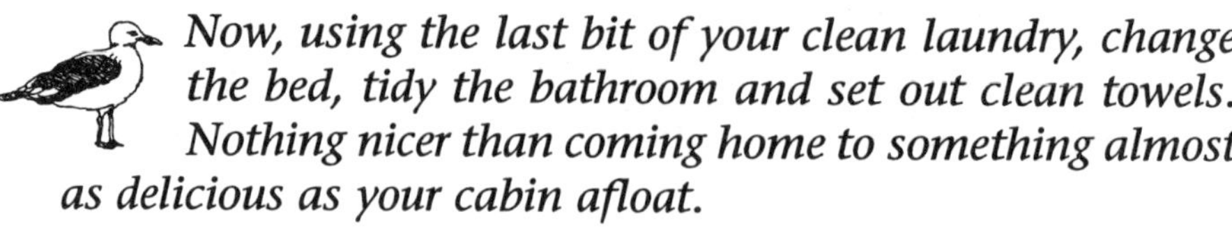

Now, using the last bit of your clean laundry, change the bed, tidy the bathroom and set out clean towels. Nothing nicer than coming home to something almost as delicious as your cabin afloat.

The Creature Comfort Bag

For our non-clothing essentials, we use a 22″ roll-aboard bag. What you will put in yours – if, indeed you take one at all – depends entirely on you. For a typical cruise, ours contains:

- A portable CD player zipped in a tidy case holding about 40 CDs. The CD player's speakers and power supply are tucked into a nylon lunch bag procured at a local drugstore. Once the CD player is hooked up, the lunch bag returns to its original purpose for off-ship picnics or snacks.
- The serious camera and associated lenses in a fanny-pack case. Depending on the destination, we may include a tripod or monopod. Plenty of film. The little camera travels in The Giant Tote Bag.

Unless you are a professional photographer, ASA 200 and 400 speeds will work for you. Make sure your flash unit and your cameras have fresh batteries. You can purchase film – usually at a reasonable price – at the photo shop aboard ship. And get your prints back in less than a day at prices comparable to those at home. Don't buy off shore film. It may be OK, datewise, but travel can take its toll.

- Binoculars (the legendary Cabela's recommends 7x50 for whales, eagles and nude beaches)
- Either a small extension cord or a cube tap, one of those devices which plugs into an outlet and offer three new plug-in outlets. Cruise ships are notorious for lack of sufficient electrical outlets.
- International power converter
- Small flashlight with fresh batteries
- Small clock
- Night light for the bathroom
- Books, including guidebooks.
- Book light for late-night reading
- Self-sealing plastic bags in various sizes
- Leather fanny-pack

- •Two plastic ponchos
- •Two small umbrellas
- •Visors or hats of choice
- •Our own diving masks and single-use underwater cameras
- •Cans or bags of mixed nuts and snack mix – you can't get those from room service.
- •Insulated coffee mugs. They hold either coffee or something sportier as we roam the decks.
- •Photocopies of prescriptions, passports and all travel documents.
- •Travelers' check information
- •A few spring-type clothes pins. Useful for the obvious but also terrific for keeping curtains closed; very useful on Alaska cruises when you can watch dusk on one side of the ship and dawn on the other in late June.

The End-Game Bag – Phase Three

This is another 22" roll-on. It's packed at the last minute because the contents – makeup, shavers, hair tools – are used at the last minute. In addition to my husband's personal ditty bag which contains both electric and blade razors, shaving cream, toothbrush, etc., I carry four makeup bags in different sizes. Of course they match.

The smallest, the "Oh, Rats!" bag, holds emergency supplies. Band-Aids, moleskin and a small pair of scissors for the inevitable blister, antibiotic ointment, Betadine, three or four pony-tail elastics to expand buttonholes late in the cruise, a seasick preventive, a sewing kit, ear plugs, small cable ties and photocopies of prescriptions and passport information.

The next smallest is called the "Fang and Claw" bag. Toenail and fingernail clippers, emery boards, an orange stick, a bottle of the current nail polish color (in a zip-top bag), nail polish remover, high-test glue to repair a broken nail, tweezers, dental floss, a topical dental anesthetic, a rubber-tipped gum stimulator and extra contact lenses.

A larger, rectangular bag, about 8"x4"x6" is the "Body Bag". Lotions, potions, styling brushes and hair sprays, body wash and puff, toothpaste, and various OTC products for anything from lower GI disorders to shipboard "dry eye" and sinus infections.

Prescription medicines should travel with you in The Giant Tote Bag at all times. If your life depends upon a particular medicine, double up and have your travel partner carry a second supply. Never leave the ship without at least two days' worth of your medicine in a bag or fanny pack.

The last bag to go in is my *real* makeup bag. Non-cruising, my makeup lives on several shelves in a bathroom closet. As I begin the tedious process of making myself presentable, I toss each bottle, pencil, case, tub or jar into the bag. When I use an eye shadow, I toss in any other colors I think I might need. I also take along a makeup base darker than the one in current use to account for sun tanning – even in Alaska.

If you change your lipstick shade as often as you change your clothes, put your lipsticks in the bag as you select accessories for your outfits.

It's a good idea to purchase "new" of essential, invisible-contents items such as mascara. You don't want to run out.

These five bags, plus the "Grease Bag" – a leak-proof case with all strengths of sun lotions and blockers, plus 100% aloe in case of too much sun – fill up the roll-on, once I've wedged in my international-class hairdryer (very small, it folds and works on different currents with the flip of a switch).

Almost every ship provides hair dryers, whether attached to the wall in the head or available from the Purser's desk. Unless you have very low-maintenance hair, take your own.

The Giant Tote Bag

Airlines are becoming pickier and pickier about carry-on bags. The Giant Tote Bag, once just a convenience, is now a necessity if you're each taking a roll-aboard. We used to sling cameras and my pocketbook over our shoulders – now the big optical guns are in the 22-incher and my purse is in the Giant Tote Bag.

Giant Tote Bag contents, which don't vary much from cruise to cruise, include:

- Travel documents – airline tickets, cruise tickets, passports, and insurance forms. Photocopy duplicates (two sets) are elsewhere in our luggage.
- Travelers' checks.
- Ship's deck plan torn from brochure.
- Fine jewelry.

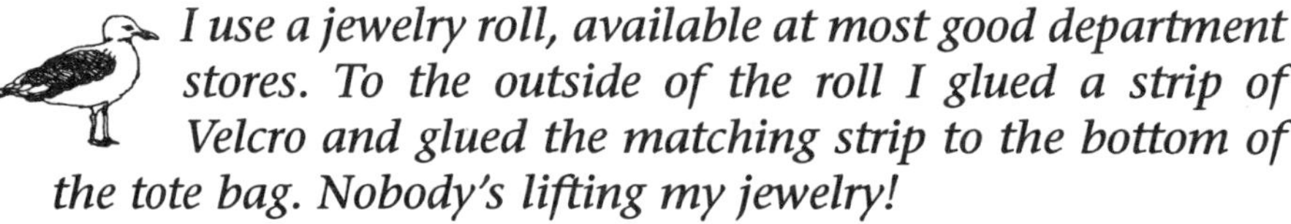

I use a jewelry roll, available at most good department stores. To the outside of the roll I glued a strip of Velcro and glued the matching strip to the bottom of the tote bag. Nobody's lifting my jewelry!

- Small camera, loaded, and a spare roll of film to capture off-the-cuff travel moments.
- Mints, travel-pack tissues, and sealed hand-wipes. High-energy snack food such as dried fruits, and stomach-fillers, usually flavored rice cakes. Bottled water.
- Address book with phone numbers and E-mail addresses.
- Inflatable neck cushions and sleep masks for long flights.
- All prescription medicines, in original containers. Photocopies of the prescriptions (two sets) are elsewhere in our luggage.
- Non-prescription medicine in the form of a good bottle of wine or a few airline-type liquor miniatures purchased from our local purveyor.
- A corkscrew.
- Books or magazines and a small notebook and pen.
- Extra pairs of eyeglasses and sunglasses, in padded cases.
- Nail clipper, needlework scissors, or small Swiss Army knife for the cable ties or shipboard arts and crafts events.

By this point, the Giant Tote Bag probably weighs at least ten pounds. However, it's a comfortable footrest when stowed under the seat in front of you.

The Great Bag on the Doorknob

It doesn't have to be on a doorknob and it doesn't have to be a bag – it's simply an early-organization repository for items that will, most likely, end up in The Giant Tote Bag, but can find transportation elsewhere. Whenever you think, "I don't want to forget ..." or, "I CAN'T forget ...", go find it and put it in The Great Bag. No, "I'll do it later," allowed. The first things to go in should be your passports or other travel ID and your tickets. After you photocopy them.

I ran out of room!

Note that the above packing plan requires only three pieces of luggage. Airlines allow four checked bags for two people. A sturdy duffel bag, preferably one with a solid bottom floor is the best catch-all-excess bag I know. Flat clothing can ride on the bottom. Put shoes and other odd-shaped items on the top layers.

But what if we're going to Alaska or on a Fall Foliage outing?

Fewer shorts, more pants. More turtlenecks, fewer T-shirts. Long sleeves instead of short. Add windsuits and hooded anorak jackets. They take up about the same amount of room. If you're visiting major cities on a Fall Foliage cruise, include casual city clothes which will work onboard. Take along a trench coat or other citified raincoat. I don't mind looking like a tourist in Barbados, but I do in Boston.

We are taking the kids. What about packing for them?

If they're older kids, the same packing methods apply. For smaller ones, put each outfit, including underwear and socks, in its own zip-top bag. If you run out of shirts, you can always buy T-shirts in port.

Your plan has most of the clothing segregated by gender. What if a bag gets lost? Does one person go naked?

Lost luggage is a rarity these days, primarily because of tightened security precautions and rampant computerization. In all my years – and millions of miles – of travel, I've had only one lost luggage problem, during the first Reagan administration. Fortunately, it was on the way home. I didn't really want to unpack, anyway, so a day's break – until the suitcases showed up – was welcome.

Be aware that the more airline connections you make on the way to your departure port, the more likely a glitch will take place. This is one of the reasons that seasoned cruisers often arrive at their port city a day early – allowing wayward luggage to catch up before they go aboard.

It's not nearly so efficient, but you can pack half-and-half in the two smaller bags. And put swimsuits and fresh shirts in the roll-aboard Creature Comfort Bag.

Other than your luggage never showing up – a most unlikely scenario – the worst thing that can happen is that Formal Night takes place before you are reunited with your belongings. The entire ship's staff will know of your travail and do everything, within reason, to accommodate you. If your sense of humor doesn't include wearing yesterday's clothes amongst everyone else's finery or spending big bucks in the boutique, they'll find you a table in an out-of-the-way corner or serve dinner in your cabin.

If you whine, threaten, complain loudly to other passengers and, generally, make a pest of yourself? The staff's cooperation level drops like a stone.

Is there anything I can do to make sure my luggage doesn't take an alternate route?

Get to the airport as early as possible, even though hanging around, eating overpriced hotdogs and drinking Cokes that can cost as much as cocktails, may be wearing. Know the three-letter code for your destination airport and, if there is one, the connecting airport. Look at the tags put on your bags to make sure they're heading the same way you are.

Early check-ins can result, for the uninitiated, in stroke-out time when the carousels begin to rumble. FILO is the rule – First In, Last Out.

The worst thing to do is to play games with your flight's departure time, screeching up to curb-side check-in half an hour from flight time, even if you do have your seat assignments and your ticket doesn't say "Check-In Required". You may have a seat – your luggage may not.

I need new luggage. What's the best?

The cheaper the better, so long as it's sturdy. If you've ever followed a suitcase on its journey from airport check-in to your cabin you know why. The airline baggage handlers and machines get the first crack, followed by their baggage handlers at the other end, the bruisers who toss the bags into the truck for the trip to the pier, the other bruisers who toss them out of the truck, then the ship's baggage boys who snag them for the last leg. Even expensive luggage needs to be replaced often with this much handling.

Our current sets came from a discount department store, on sale. There isn't a lot of room to store luggage on a cruise ship, so all the better to purchase your bags in descending sizes (26", 24", 22") so they'll nest inside each other under your bed.

Why do we have to put the ship's tags on our luggage before we leave home? Doesn't it confuse the people at the airline?

If you didn't put them on before you left home, your luggage would be at the airport, unclaimed, as your ship sailed out to sea. The bruisers and ship's baggage boys need them and you'll need them, too, when you claim your bags at trip's end. Once you've checked in with the airline, unless you have to clear customs at your departure port, you won't see your suitcases again until you're on the ship.

If you book your own transportation, you are responsible for getting yourself – and your luggage – to the pier. Tags on. The porters know what to do.

When are you going to spill about those electrical cable ties?

Right now. If your luggage features adorable little padlocks with tiny little keys, you *need* cable ties. Thread them through the openings where the little padlock's hasp would otherwise go and ratchet them down. Clip off any excess plastic. The ties are almost invisible and will foil all but the most sophisticated attempts to break into your suitcases. There's the added comfort factor of knowing your luggage won't unzip itself on an airport carousel, revealing to the world that you wear flannel pajamas imprinted with leaping purple frogs.

If you forget the nail clipper or embroidery scissors to sever the ties once in your cabin, there's probably a corkscrew next to the ice bucket if you forgot yours. It has a small, dull knife as part of the apparatus. It works. Slowly.

Speaking of things electrical, shouldn't I take my travel iron?

No. Ships are very clear on the use of irons (except in the laundry room, if there is one), and for good reason. It's too easy to iron, using your bed as the ironing board, and forget to turn off the iron in your haste to begin the next activity. This could mean that you, just trying to look nice, set your ship on fire. Evening ruined.

Steamers, which use less power, are allowable but, if you use the Cruise Control packing method, you won't need either.

Laundry Room?

Believe it or not, some ships on some cruise lines allow you to forget that you're on vacation. You can do your own laundry! If your ship has a laundry room and you intend to use it, stash some secure plastic bags full of your favorite powdered detergent (or small jars of liquid) in your Creature Comfort Bag.

What kind of "amenities" can I expect in our bathroom?

It depends on your cruise line. Low-end, a bar or two of low-end soap. As you climb the ladder to more upscale ships, more – and more top-drawer – bathroom goodies are offered. On a mainstream, mid-line ship, expect shampoo, conditioner, and hand lotion. Moving up, you'll find shower caps, shoe horns, liquid body wash, and sewing kits.

As a creature of habit, I always pack my own shampoo, lotions and potions.

Can I "steal" those goodies to take home?

Sure. Enough previous passengers have done it so the projected cost is already built into your cruise fare. Don't be greedy.

What am I forgetting?

Pictures of the kids, grandkids, and assorted family pets. Business cards to exchange with other people who have business cards. A calculator for foreign currency exchange rates. Look in The Great Bag to see if there is anything left in the bottom.

Chapter Three

Welcome Aboard

There she is. Your ship. Even the most seasoned cruisers get a thrill out of seeing her alongside in the departure port. In this chapter, we'll walk up the gangway, find our way around the ship, unpack, meet the staff, and figure out what they're up to. This chapter also includes tips on tipping.

That Kodak Moment

Go ahead and smile at the cute young person wielding a camera at the end of the gangplank – even though this photo probably won't be a keeper. I've always thought the photo ploy was a clever way to space out passengers as they boarded because I've never seen a boarding photo – of me – that wouldn't scare the horses. Depending upon the port and the cruise line you may or may not go through a weapons detector, *a la* airport, on your way to the ship.

In addition to the photographer, you'll probably be greeted by a swirl of ship's officers and entertainers before a smiling person escorts you to your cabin. You have probably already surrendered your carry-on bags and are left only with The Giant Tote Bag. Your cruise documents settled, immediately, to the bottom of The Giant Tote Bag. What *is* your cabin number?

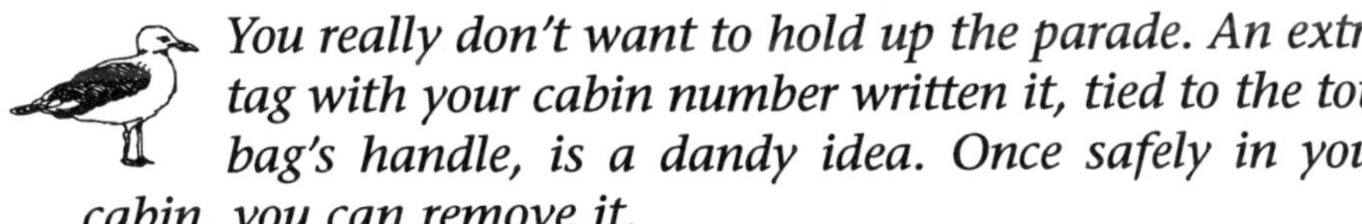

You really don't want to hold up the parade. An extra tag with your cabin number written it, tied to the tote bag's handle, is a dandy idea. Once safely in your cabin, you can remove it.

Cabin Fever

It is unlikely that your luggage beat you to your cabin. Whether you're in the smallest of inside cabins or the Owner's Suite, this is the time to pre-organize your days and nights to come. You know what you brought with you – now figure out where you're going to put it.

With the exception of the tux jacket and sports coat, everything that needs to hang is already on a hanger. Check the closets. On some ships, the supply of wooden hangers is so generous that there's no room for your own hanging clothes. Find the laundry bag (usually in the bottom of the closet) and stash the wooden hangers in it. You can give the package to your steward/ess later.

You will notice an ice bucket somewhere in the cabin. If you are so inclined, now is the time to reach into The Giant Tote Bag for the nice Chardonnay or those little airline-type bottles you purchased at your local purveyor of spirits. (Shipboard liquor policies are discussed in Chapter 5.) Suitably relaxed, read the ship's daily newspaper outlining the sailaway events.

About now, your smiling cabin steward/ess arrives to welcome you aboard. (Henceforth, "steward" means both men and women.) These folks will do almost anything for you, happily and in hopes of an excellent tip. This is the time to tell the steward about any special requirements you have – more pillows, a full ice bucket all the time, an extra ashtray.

Go Safely

If your cabin has a safe – and most do, these days – now is the time to stash your good jewelry, your wallets and credit cards, your cash, passports, and your cruise documents. All you need aboard ship is your "sail-and-spend" ID card, probably given to you at check-in or, otherwise, awaited you in your cabin. It may also be your room key.

Cabin safes are often operated by a magnetic stripe card. Some people bring along a library card or supermarket identification card rather than using an active credit card to operate the safe. If you're using the safe to protect your credit cards, you can't lock up the one that operates the safe.

Failing a safe, or if you're traveling with a lot of money ($10,000 is the usual maximum for purposes of customs) or some exceptionally expensive jewelry, your first stop is the Purser's office. The staff will gladly activate your sail-and-spend card – take the credit card you wish to use for your final accounting along – and provide a lock box. Even if you don't want a lock box, the Purser's Desk is a good place to start.

Getting Your Sea Legs

This has nothing to do with perambulation while the ship is at sea. It has everything to do with finding your way around the ship, from one end to the other, and from deck to deck. Remember the deck plan in your brochure? The one you were supposed to tear out? Did you remember to bring it along? If you didn't, ask the Purser's staff for one.

Back in the cabin, you should have noticed a little card assigning you to either Main or Late Seating for dinner as well as a table number. The dining room captains, under the control of either the maitre d' or the food and beverage manager (sometimes both) are available outside the dining room – or in another designated location – for any necessary changes.

You'll be finding the dining room again and again on this cruise, so make it your first stop, whether or not you have a complaint. For the truly compulsive, you can return to your cabin first and map out the best route.

The empty dining room means something important – food is being served somewhere else, probably in the casual dining room, which is usually on the pool deck, and on the pool deck itself. A corollary to this logic is: where there's food, there are people. Unless you're starving, now's the time to take a leisurely stroll through the public rooms. And the time to make note of the location of less public rooms – the rest rooms.

Let's Talk Nauti(cal)

A ship is always "she". And she has two ends – the pointy one and the round one. The pointy one is called the bow and the round one is called the stern. Ships also have two sides – port and starboard. If you're standing, looking toward the pointy end, port is on your left. It's easy to remember – port has the same number of letters as left.

It sounds silly, but in these days of mega-liners where you can't see from one end to the other, it's not a bad idea to stand in the door of your cabin and repeat, making an appropriate hand signal if you want, "bow", "stern." Or, "pointy", "round."

At departure, the ship may be "dressed" with nautical pennants strung from bow to stern. Notice the flags she's flying. In port, she flies three – the country of registry, the owner's flag, and the flag of the port country.

On a port-intensive cruise, take a photo of the mast with flags flying at every stop. Very cool in the photo album.

Those huge ropes you see holding her steady, or any ropes for that matter, are always called lines. In the case of lines this size, they're hawsers. The things they're tied to are called bollards.

When you're outside on a ship, you're on a weather deck. And if you ever feel the slightest bit seasick, a weather deck is where you want to be. Below (inside) you may feel hemmed in by the overhead (ceiling) and the bulkheads (walls).

Nobody's going to keelhaul you (that means tying you to a line and dragging you under the ship – the keel being the bottommost point of the ship) if you say front, back, right, left and ropes. But you may be called a lubber by an old Navy guy if you use the word "boat" instead of "ship." Boats are those orange things that hang on davits on the sides of your ship. You can recognize the Navy guys by their snappy caps.

A Case of the Grip

By now, your luggage should be in the vicinity of your cabin. If you were extremely nice to your cabin steward, it's inside your cabin. Otherwise, it's outside and you can haul it in yourself.

Two people should never try to unpack at the same time. If you're traveling with a domestic familiar, park him/her as far away from your base of unpacking operations as possible. If you're traveling with a friend, decide who goes first.

Put the largest suitcase, the one with all the hanging clothes, on the foot of the bed, close to the closet. Take everything out and hang it up. Elapsed time: three minutes, tops.

It doesn't make much difference which of the two 24" bags are next up. You already know where everything's going. Put shoes, belts, evening bags, and other small stuff to one side on the bed. Everything else goes to its preplanned location. Stash one 24" bag inside the 26" bag. Elapsed time: ten minutes if you take it slow.

Open the Creature Comfort Bag and remove the hanging shoe bag. Hang it, and stuff the small stuff into it. Elapsed time: two minutes.

Next up, the Last Minute Bag. Truck all the tidy little cases into the bathroom ("head" in nauti-terms) and arrange them in order of importance. Put that bag inside the 26" and 24", zip and kick under the bed. Kick the other 24" under, as well. Elapsed time: five minutes, max.

Now you can take your time with the Creature Comfort Bag, figuring out what goes where and why it does. When you're finished with those important arrangements, put the Creature Comfort Bag under the bed, solo. It just became an extra drawer, a souvenir repository or a laundry basket.

At this point, you're only missing two essentials – and it's your job to go out and find them. One is what the British call a "tooth mug". It's a bathroom glass, more or less, and you already have two – but you want one more to store your toothbrushes and toothpaste. Stewards just cannot understand the need for a third. Ask a bartender.

The other essential is "The Container". Over time, I've liberated soup bowls from dining tables and large brandy snifters from bars, but nothing works quite so well as a coin cup from the casino. The Container holds all the flotsam and jetsam which would otherwise take over your cabin – eyeglasses, casino chips, sail-and-spend cards, bar receipts, last night's earrings, anything you want to be able to get your hands on quickly, or which would get lost or create a mess.

Hello, Mae West

With any luck, it's not going to be a bumpy ride, but you must participate in the SOLAS (Safety of Life at Sea) drill. You'll learn your muster point in case of emergency and be instructed about the use of your life preserver and the procedures for boarding the life boats. (Please don't blow the whistle attached to your life vest.)

Only three ships which weren't torpedoed (*Lusitania*) have sunk during regular passenger service in the 20th century – *Titanic*, *Andrea Doria*, and *Sun Vista* (*Sun Vista* with no loss of life, thanks to SOLAS regulations), but others have been evacuated. Pay attention and don't worry – everyone else looks as silly as you do.

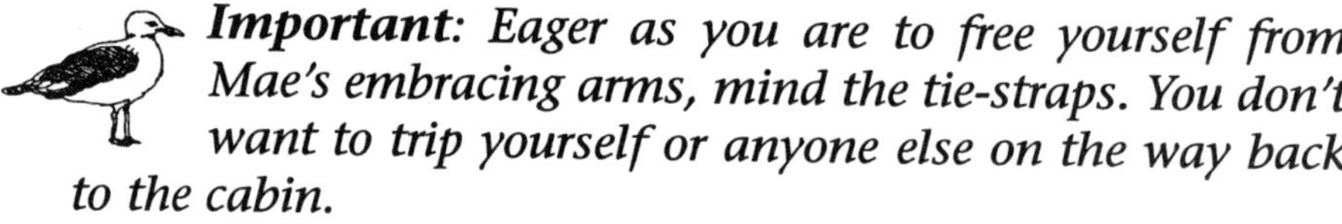

***Important:** Eager as you are to free yourself from Mae's embracing arms, mind the tie-straps. You don't want to trip yourself or anyone else on the way back to the cabin.*

Take the drill seriously and remember that your muster point for the drill might not be the same in case of a real emergency. Once back in your cabin, give some thought to the essentials you'd take with you in case of an evacuation. Essential prescription drugs should be at the top of the list, followed by passports, credit cards, and money. Make a plan to raid the bathroom of drugs, and the safe of essential documents, cash, and jewelry. A fanny pack should hold it all.

Who's Driving the Boat?

You'll get the chance to shake hands with the Captain on the first Formal Night. Don't ask him that question – ten people already have and another ten are waiting to do so. The Captain is technically referred to as the Master of the vessel. He and his officers are called the bridge staff. Usually, the Captain introduces the top staff members at the cocktail party after the handshaking.

Tips on Tipping

Any good-sized ship has a population of at least two to three thousand, both passengers and crew. The easiest way to sort out the hierarchy of non-officer crew is to split them into those you see and those you usually don't see. The invisible crew members are laundry workers, maintenance people, kitchen help, and mechanics.

Those you see are mostly those expecting tips. In the dining room, you'll find the maitre d', a number of captains overseeing individual sections of the dining room, and waiters and busboys (sometime called assistant waiters) who serve a small number of tables. The *sommelier* (wine steward) will be around. No tip necessary for him or her, a percentage of the cost of the bottle is added to the check. A good sommelier – one who really knows wine and makes excellent suggestions – gets a tip from us.

If you like a particular wine well enough that you'd buy it for home, ask the sommelier to soak off the label.

Bartenders and cocktail waitstaff are also on the auto-tip method, which may be why they're always smiling.

In the casino, it's considered to be sporting to tip the dealer or croupier after a significant win. A chip or two of the value you were playing with will do.

You'll be seeing as much of your cabin steward as you will your waiter. You can pre-tip a portion ($10, perhaps?) of the amount you've set aside. This will definitely get attention. Keep a few dollar bills in The Container to tip the cheerful person who does the morning coffee service or provides other goodies from room service.

Most cruise lines provide you with a set of tipping guidelines pre-departure. It's a good idea to set your estimated tip money aside on the first day, just so you won't be caught short at trip's end. The crew members who are routinely tipped make very little other money, sometimes none, and depend on tips for their livelihood, sending most of it back home to their families.

In general, you'll tip your waiter and cabin steward from the same *per diem* base, then give half the amount of the waiter's tip to the busboy. It's up to you whether to tip the room captain overseeing your section or the maitre d'. If they've performed a special service, definitely. Otherwise, it's your call.

One mainstream cruise line advertises, "Tipping not required." It's not required, but do it anyway if you find yourself on a *'dam* (Holland America) ship. Research current tipping guidelines from cruising friends or on cruise-related websites, including Porthole.com. Tip bar personnel when you receive your drinks. One or two dollars per pair of drinks is fine.

There are ships where tipping is not allowed. And they're serious about it. If you're fortunate enough to find yourself on one of these deluxe vessels, you'll have the dilemma of figuring out a way to say "Thank you" without using hard currency.

On one cruise, we took along a T-shirt from the Atlanta Olympics, figuring it would suit either sex. On another, when we knew that all the cabin staff were young women, we took five dozen homemade brownies – my daughter's suggestion. A super-size box of Jelly Bellies was also appreciated. One thing we've not yet tried is hitting a hip record store and asking for the hottest-selling CD.

Never, ever, offer to tip any uniformed officer or member of the Cruise Director's staff. If someone performs an extra-special service, sit down in your cabin and, using the ship's notepaper, write a thank you note. And a note of commendation to his or her superior.

What happens if I don't eat dinner in the main dining room every night? Do I deduct from the waiter's tip?

No. The waiters in alternative dining rooms are compensated for not being in the main dining room during that particular sailing, often on a tip-share basis with the main dining room waiters. The only excuse for not tipping the waiter? He's a lousy waiter. If that's the case, take it up with the room captain or maitre d'. But don't take it out on the assistant waiter/busboy if he's done a good job.

We ate in an alternative restaurant, and they asked for a $5 service charge. What's that about?

On some cruise lines, the alternative restaurants are staffed by the same people all the time, rather than on a rotating basis, so the financial arrangements are a bit different. You still owe your regular waiter his tip – he was there, but you weren't.

We're taking our two children, six and eight years old, on a cruise. We don't have to tip the same for them as we do for us, do we?

Yes. It might even be nice to tip more. If you already have two children, you know that the amount of work associated with them has nothing to do with the amount of food they eat or the amount of space they take up. The fare reduction for third and fourth people in the same cabin has no relationship to the work that's done for those third and fourth persons and certainly no relationship to the number of seats they occupy in the dining room.

We changed tables halfway through the cruise to sit with new friends. We changed waiters, too. How do we tip?

If it was halfway, half-and-half is fair.

I really do want to know who's driving the boat.

At sea, it's probably a computer (autopilot), working together with the watch officer and helmsman close at hand. Coming into or departing from port, a helmsman steers the ship under the guidance of a local pilot who is intimately familiar with the waters. It's the Captain and his First Officer doing the driving right at the pier. You can see them on the pier side fly bridge as the ship arrives and departs.

Uh-oh. Our cabin has twin beds and we like to ... well ... you know.

If the survey done by *Cosmopolitan* magazine a few years ago is anywhere near accurate, "well ... you know" is an extremely popular shipboard activity. Just ask your steward to move the beds together. Thy will be done.

Of course, if the beds are already together and you wish them separated, just ask.

What if I forget something?

You are not doomed. The ship's gift shop carries essential toiletries, over-the-counter type medicines and hygiene needs. And there's always the next port. The gift shop is not open in port, so plan ahead.

If you use the Cruise Control method of packing, the chances of forgetting something are almost non-existent.

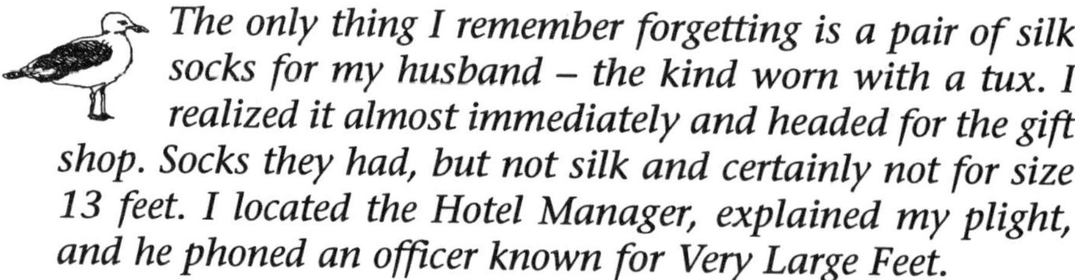

The only thing I remember forgetting is a pair of silk socks for my husband – the kind worn with a tux. I realized it almost immediately and headed for the gift shop. Socks they had, but not silk and certainly not for size 13 feet. I located the Hotel Manager, explained my plight, and he phoned an officer known for Very Large Feet.

Anything else we should be doing on our first day aboard?

If you want a salon appointment for hair, nails, or other beauty treatments before the Captain's gala, make it immediately upon boarding. And you probably don't want to miss sailaway.

Sailaway?

That's when your ship leaves port. Bands are probably playing, waiters are certainly offering libations, and most people prefer to be on a weather deck to take in the total sensation. As a general rule, sailaway, whether from your embarkation port or ports along the way, is in the afternoon or early evening. It's a much better time to take photos than the often horribly early hour when the ship makes port.

Chapter Four

One Day At A Time

There are two sorts of days on a cruise – at-sea days and in-port days. At sea, the ship buzzes with activity; in most ports, things are a little slower aboard as the casino and shops must be closed and most people pelt down the gangway for a new experience. In this chapter, we'll walk through the days and dance the nights away.

All at Sea

Many people like to start an at-sea day with a lazy room service breakfast. Why not? You're not going anywhere. The room service person also serves as a handy alarm clock. On some ships, you receive a warning phone call. On others, it's just a knock.

Even before leaving your cabin you can keep up to date on the latest world events. Most ships are equipped with the newest satellite technology and pipe CNN International into the cabin television set. For those who can't start the day without the morning newspaper, you can read the *TimesFax* which was slipped under your door in the wee small hours. *TimesFax* is a service of the *New York Times* with the latest national and international news, business news, sports and weather in a condensed format. It even includes the famous *NewYork Times* crossword puzzle (edited by our friend Will Shortz, whose name rebus is WILLz. Get it? That may be a question in the Daily Quiz.)

Your cabin television has only a few channels. There are no local stations while at sea, but there is satellite television. CNN International seems to be a staple as well as one of the sports networks. You can also watch movies in your cabin, see a replay of yesterday's port lecture, watch the endlessly repeated safety lecture, or tune in to the "Bridge Cam." The camera on the bridge gives you a fascinating view of the empty ocean while you are at sea or the container ship in front of you in port. As entertainment, the bridge camera is somewhat akin to watching moss grow.

Traditional get-dressed-before-you-eat breakfasts are usually found in both the main dining room and the casual restaurant area. In the main dining room, there are two seatings and you will usually be seated at your assigned table. This is a good time to take a close look at the ship's daily newspaper, if you haven't already done so, to choose your activities for the day. You've probably already missed sunrise coffee and the brisk around-the-deck-X-times-equals-a-mile walk event.

Even though meals are usually served buffet-style in the casual restaurant, look around for a chef doing custom omelets at breakfast and pasta dishes at lunchtime.

The ship's shops are open and you'll have a chance to look at (and purchase) the photo taken as you boarded. If it's perfectly awful – and ours always are – the photo shop people provide a handy location to pitch it. You can also pitch a few coins into the slots – the *cha-ching* usually starts before noon with table games opening later in the day.

Activities range from the benign (napkin folding) to the raucous (pool games overseen by the Cruise Director's staff) or the mildly competitive (team trivia). The ship's beauty salon is operating at warp speed on the first day at sea because it usually coincides with the Captain's Welcome Aboard cocktail party.

If you want hair styled, body massaged, or a facial before the Captain's party, make your reservation IMMEDIATELY when you board the ship.

There's no hard-and-fast list of activities that applies to every cruise ship, but you can usually expect something like this:

- Sports equipment available all day
- Daily Trivia Quiz
- Walk-a-Mile
- Step Aerobics Class
- Stretch and Relax Class
- Port Talk

- Library is open
- Shore Excursion Talk
- Ping Pong Tournament
- Trapshooting
- Team Trivia
- Fashion Show
- Shuffleboard (really!)
- Service club meetings
- Friends of Bill W.
- BINGO!
- Perfume seminar
- Wine tasting
- Cooking demonstration
- Napkin folding
- Ballroom/Line dancing class
- Poolside horseracing
- Casino lessons
- Bridge
- Basketball
- Pool Olympics
- Arts & crafts
- Golf putting or driving
- Tea music

Be warned, the time slots are scheduled tightly and everything on a cruise ship seems to start on time, if not a couple of minutes before.

Lunch follows the same seating plan in the main dining room as breakfast. If you're not dressed for the dining room or hate to miss a minute of power-tanning, the casual restaurant requires only shoes and a cover-up – the predictable burgers-and-dogs grill on the pool deck doesn't even ask that.

The evening after your first full day at sea will probably be a Formal Night, so plan your getting-ready time carefully, especially if you wish to take advantage of the formal photos the ship's shutterbugs are more than willing to take, develop and sell.

Don't feel shy about asking the camera person to click twice.

A Masterful Gesture – The Captain's Welcome Aboard Party

For an hour or so before each dinner seating, the Captain greets his guests at the door to the main show lounge. There's usually a photographer snapping away as each passenger or couple touches greatness. A band plays easy-dancing music; cocktails are served.

If the Captain seems amenable to something more than a nod and a handshake, the appropriate comment is, "A pleasure to be aboard." If it feels good, you can tack a "Sir" on the end of that.

Handshakes accomplished, the Captain takes the stage and, depending upon his facility with English, gives either a short or shorter speech of welcome. He introduces the ship's officers and senior staff and bids everyone *bon voyage.* Then it's time for dinner. *Bon appetit.*

Cocktail-wise, this may be the only free drink you get on your cruise. And whatever the waiter or waitress has on his or her tray is what's available at that moment. The drinks are usually weak and warm. I recommend champagne.

After dinner, there are still more choices: hitting the show lounge for an extravaganza – for the evening's big deal entertainment – an after-dinner drink in a quiet corner (if you can find one) – dancing, listening and people watching in other lounges – and, late-night, the disco fires up.

Land Ho!

In port, breakfast and lunch in the main dining room are open seating – just show up, be seated and be served. The casual and poolside offerings are the same as yesterday's.

The ship's shops are closed, the casino isn't in operation, and you have two choices: go ashore or stay onboard. If going ashore, there are two more choices: take a shore excursion offered by the ship or freelance. Both have their charms. An Official Shore Excursion is charged to your on-board account, the providers have been vetted and approved by the cruise line, and the ship won't leave without you if the bus happens to break down.

Ship's Trips – Organized Shore Excursions

Experienced cruisers know that for practically any excursion you can purchase on board, a similar one is cheaper once you get down the gangway. However, if there's something you have your heart set on, shaving a few bucks isn't worth the disappointment if you can't manage to make pier-side arrangements.

Cruise staffers are energetic about convincing you to book shore excursions aboard. Some aren't particularly subtle, hinting of dangers – including the ship leaving without you – if you choose to freelance. One way to avoid these tactics is to skip the port lecture.

In port, passengers with already-arranged ship's trips usually receive the courtesy of being first ashore. Bus passes are delivered to your cabin the night before the excursion. Listen carefully for announcements about assembly locations, when to board your bus and which deck will be used for debarking. Some tours are so popular that one bus isn't enough. Sometimes it's first-come, first-served on the bus fleet, other times your bus pass will be color-coded and you must find your matching bus. As a general rule in a multi-bus situation, once you're on a bus it's yours. Drivers count noses before leaving a stop and if noses are missing, everyone waits. Usually. Don't test this rule. And don't test your co-passengers' patience by dawdling.

Once aboard the bus and underway, either the driver or a guide is happy to dish local information, point out sights along the way to your destination, and answer questions.

If you're the sort of person who asks a lot of questions or doesn't want to miss anything, try to snag a seat toward the front of the bus.

If your excursion is just a ride into town or another location, you're on your own for lunch. If it's an all-day, multi-stop trip, lunch will probably be included. Check the brochure

There's no rule against ordering sandwiches from room service, scoring fruit and yogurt from the breakfast buffet, and putting your picnic in the Giant Tote Bag unless there is a rule. And in some ports, that is the case. However, I have never seen any official types inspect tote bags, giant or otherwise, for contraband bananas.

Certain to be included in the all-day activity is a scheduled *shopportunity.* The storekeepers know they have a captive audience and the prices generally reflect it. Don't be annoyed if one of your tablemates freelanced and purchased the same shawl or handicraft for half the price.

Tipping either driver or driver and guide is a matter of personal discretion. Some drivers/guides are a bit more aggressive than others. Placing gaily wrapped coffee cans or the like with "Thank You" printed on them near the door is usually a clue as to their desires. A perfectly acceptable scale is $1 per person for a half day, $2 for a full day unless the driver/guide has been outstanding.

Born Free – Expensive Now

Freelancing isn't for everyone. A sense of adventure, a good guidebook, and local currency for public transportation are the only requirements. In many popular ports, you don't even need the guidebook and U.S. dollars are accepted for everything.

In some countries where U.S. dollars are freely accepted, crumpled, torn or otherwise mutilated U.S.

dollars aren't. Mexico is notorious for this. When you hit your local bank for travel cash, ask for new money.

Probably the best resource for freelancers is the Internet. It's hard to find a vacation destination that doesn't have a tourist bureau presence on the Internet and, usually, you'll find a host of other sites by means of a simple search. Don't overlook travel areas and clubs on the various services. You'll find people there who have, literally, "been there and done that." They're delighted to answer questions and share their experiences. Every now and then you'll get a bum steer (I'm still annoyed about a restaurant recommendation in Hong Kong) but for the most part the advice is solid and reliable. Finding a wonderful small hotel near Puerta Vallarta at $25 per night more than made up for the Hong Kong dinner.

The Number One challenge to freelancers is transportation, whether it's renting a car or a scooter, hiring a van or a taxi complete with driver, conquering the public transportation system or simply finding your way on foot. The shore excursion brochure should give you a few ideas about what you might want to do in a particular port; the ship's newspaper should offer still more information.

If all you crave is a trip into town or being delivered to a beach, almost any driver will do. If you're interesting in touring, it's more important to determine whether or not you have a common language with the driver/guide.

If you ask a prospective driver if the island got a lot of snow last week and he answers, "Yes! Very yes!" keep looking.

"Clubbing up" to share a van or a cab with others is cost-effective – half the price or less – and double or more the fun. Just make sure you've negotiated the price ahead of time and that the driver understands he will be paid once you're safely back at the pier.

All drivers-for-hire, at least in the Caribbean, come from extremely large families. Their cousins, nephews, brothers and uncles own numerous restaurants and many stores, offering the best food and the hottest bargains on the island. Your driver will be happy to take you to any or all of them.

Don't let your driver tell you that you must do one thing or another. If you don't want to visit the rope factory or the alligator hatchery, even if they are the pride of the island, just say so. Your shipmates on the planned excursions have to suffer through them – you don't. A good plan is to ask the driver for an orientation tour first. Then you can decide what to do next – go back to the falls, hit the third beach along the way, or visit that little craft market next door to the church that you also want to visit.

When you scatter – shopping, for example – make sure everyone has a watch and knows the rendezvous place and time. The very best drivers/guides find a place to sit nearby the meeting spot and are available for serious shopping negotiations if there's a language barrier with a vendor, who's probably your driver's cousin, anyway.

If you've hired your driver for the day, you will probably stop for lunch. It's a courtesy to invite your driver to join you and pick up his tab. It's highly unlikely he will accept but, if you've all been getting along famously, you may insist or he may happily agree. Don't be quite so generous with your invitation if you're stopping for a serious margarita fix. Most drivers choose to hang with their relatives while you're enjoying your meal or drinks.

Back at the ship, it's time to shower off the sand and the shopping dust before dinner – generally a casual night if the port stop was long, possibly informal if sailaway is at four o'clock.

Sea Days Onboard

Maybe you've been to a port twenty times before. Maybe the port doesn't interest you. Maybe you have a cold or an attitude and just plain want to stay in one place. The pace of activities aboard slows to a crawl once almost everyone else has gone ashore. It's not impossible that the main dining room will be closed and the only lunch available will be in the casual restaurant or on the pool deck.

You are not required to get off the ship. More important, especially if traveling with a domestic partner, is that you don't have to be joined at the hip. You aren't at home, why on a cruise? If one person wants to laze around and the other is hot for hiking to the top of the local volcano, laze on and hike on. It will give you fodder for dinner conversation.

Are the ship's shore excursions really a rip-off?

Most emphatically, NO. They are more expensive than an almost identical tour you can pick up on the pier but they have several advantages. You are with an "official" group at all times, the service is door-to-door, everything is done for you, and all you have to do is get on and off the bus. The comfort and security level is high; that's important to a lot of people. And the ship really will not leave without you.

We want to freelance. What if the ship does leave without us?

The smartest thing to do is make sure your plans include the worst possible thing that could happen as far as possible from the ship – then build that time into your return schedule. Drivers are particularly sensitive to time constraints.

We've only known people to miss the boat twice – both times in Bermuda when our ship was docked a good distance from downtown Hamilton and passengers had to depend on the ship's tender, the commuter ferry, or the local buses. They were shopping, lost track of time, and missed the last opportunity to get to the ship on time. Not surprisingly, in each instance there was a gentleman with a fast boat who offered, for a significant sum of money, to catch the ship. We have always wondered whether or not he took credit cards.

Other than parting with many monies, rejoining the ship from a small boat alongside is not for the faint of heart. If you've ever watched the harbor pilots shinny up those flimsy rope ladders, that's how you have to board. No gangplanks at sea.

Like everything else on ships, the rope ladder has a name – it's a Jacob's Ladder. If you ever get the chance to climb one, you'll know why people wrote hymns about them.

If you miss the ship, another plan is to stay overnight in port and charter an airplane or find a commercial flight and meet your ship at the next port.

What about money when we're ashore? And shopping? And bargaining?

These questions are so important they have their own chapter, Chapter 6.

What if we want to tour around, then go to a beach, and then go shopping all in the same day?

Get an early start. Women can wear sundresses or other accommodating outfits over bathing suits, underwear (in a plastic bag) goes into the Giant Tote Bag. Men can wear a shirt and a bathing suit – so long as it's not a Speedo type – with shorts and underwear also in the Giant Tote Bag. Wet bathing suits, once used, go into the leakproof bags that held the dry clothes. Don't forget the suntan lotion, either the entire Grease Bag or the SPF *du jour*.

Beach Towels?

The ship provides them, signed out to your cabin account. Either you order them from your cabin steward or collect them as you debark. But if you lose one, you'll find out just how expensive large, plain towels can be. Don't be shy about asking for more than one.

Anything else?

Sunglasses, visor, a hairbrush to share, wet-wipes for hands, a small pack of tissues in case of ill-equipped restrooms, bottled water, and your official ship's ID card.

Is there any way of telling which portside driver is the best?

They all are. Just ask them. In some ports, there are drivers with an "official" designation, which usually indicates their vehicle is safe and they have either attended or passed a course on guiding. Look for a sticker in the window or on the license plate. Even better, ask your Cruise Director what official notification to look for before you get off the ship.

Why should we pay a driver to hang around all day if all we're going to do is go to the beach?

Don't. Just make sure you set a time for him to pick you up for the return journey. He'll probably insist on payment when he drops you off; that's only fair. Sometimes people change their minds and find other transportation back to the ship.

What about tips for private drivers?

Nice, but not necessary if they own their own vehicles and are self-employed.

What happens if I forget my ship's ID card?

It depends on the ship and the port. Some cruise lines check for them as you debark, which lessens the chances of forgetting. The newer ships have instituted an electronic system that allows you to swipe your combination sail-and-spend/cabin key card through a magnetic-strip reader much like an ATM machine as you get on and off the ship. In some ports, you must go through a mini-customs with local officials checking your ID as you get off. But if you do forget your ID – or it's lost or stolen – you probably will not be denied boarding. On the smaller, more intimate ships, the staff probably recognizes you as one of their passengers. On one of the large mega-liners you will become one of the security staff's new best friends while they check your *bona fides.*

Some ships allow passengers to come and go at will, just flashing a boarding card on your way in. Other ships want to know who is on board and who is ashore and have methods for checking you out and checking you in. Those methods range from high tech computer systems to a security officer with a clipboard standing at the gangway writing down cabin numbers as you get off and on.

How I spent my day

50

EAT, DRINK AND BE MERRY

If there's a single word synonymous with "cruise", it's probably more likely to be "food" than "water". The first question civilians – and experienced cruisers – ask when you return home is, "How was the food?" My years of reading cruise reviews on the Internet bear this out – more space is given to describing and critiquing meals than any other part of the cruise experience.

In this chapter, we'll give food – and its companion, drink – the attention it so richly deserves.

The Main Dining Room

Traditionally the centerpiece of shipboard cuisine, the main dining room defines the overall quality of the dining experience. When a cruiser says, "Dinners were fine, but breakfast and lunch didn't do much for me," it's a good bet that cruiser didn't take those meals in the Main Dining Room.

The Main Dining Room (some larger ships have more than one) is a quiet land of floral arrangements, soft music, glittering crystal, tasteful china, shining silver, and enough linen to cover your average football field. It's also the place where more staff competes for your tip dollar than anywhere else on the ship. (Your room steward comes in a distant second.)

There's a strict staff/crew hierarchy that varies from cruise line to cruise line. As an example, the Staff Captain reports to the Captain. The Hotel Manager reports to the Staff Captain. The Maitre d' reports to the Hotel and Restaurant Manager, who reports to the Staff Captain. Room Captains report to the Maitre d'. Waiters serve under the watchful eye of Room Captains, and busboys – or assistant waiters – serve, in turn, the waiters.

Your first visit to the dining room is always a bit chaotic as everyone finds the proper table for the first time. Don't forget your table assignment card. And, if you wish to look every bit the world cruiser, wait about ten minutes from the time the meal is called to enter the dining room on the first night. The Main Dining Room staff will be grateful that you're not part of the initial flesh press and you'll have a moment to make a good first impression, which will serve you well as the cruise goes on.

Thou Preparest a Table Before Me

Now for the fun part. If you're seated at anything but a table for two – a four, a six, an eight, a ten – will your tablemates be friends or enemies? Most cruisers enjoy meeting new people – breaking bread together is one of the best ways to get to know others.

There's no delicate way to say it. Sometimes you'll be saddled with tablemates who offend your sensibilities for one reason or another. Maybe it's wardrobe, maybe it's hygiene or maybe it's boorish behavior. Perhaps you simply have nothing in common. If they're drinking beer and talking about motorcycles and you're drinking wine and discussing Restoration novels, there may be a bit of tension around the groaning board. Do not take this to the Chaplain. Or the Captain. Take it directly to the maitre d', preferably with some "salad" (a $10 or $20) in your pocket to pass, with extreme discretion, into his waiting hand when you ask for a change of tables.

We were once seated at a table for four with a couple from Paris. They had very little English, my husband's high school French was just that, and I was on another continent entirely. The first night's dinner was extremely awkward and, we found out later, both couples considered asking for a change of table. As it turned out, the four of us dined with the Captain the next night – putting off the decision – and, after enough wine, their English and my husband's French improved dramatically. We swapped addresses at the end of the cruise.

It's also possible that you'll be the victim of The Waiter from Hell. There's at least one in every dining room and the staff knows who he is or they are. They tend to serve tables closer to the center – thus, under watchful eyes at all times – and serve fewer tables. The Waiter from Hell may be brand-new and unsure of what he's doing. He may be on his last or next-to-last cruise under his current contract and can't wait to get home. He may have broken up with his shipboard lover or received a letter from home that made him unhappy. Who knows?

You do not have to tolerate The Waiter From Hell.

This request for a change does not require taking salad to the maitre d'. He should give you money for pointing out problems in his dining room. Don't pull any punches. Explain what the waiter did or didn't do that drove you to such extreme measures. Not only will the miscreant be reprimanded, he'll lose your tip money, which probably hurts even worse. But remember the busboy. He doesn't deserve punishment, even if the waiter does.

Personally, we tend to cut new waiters a bit of a break but won't tolerate the surly or those with other attitude problems. We are also sympathetic to the busboys who, because of their waiter bosses, miss out on tippage. Once on a jam-packed cruise where a waiter station move wasn't possible, the Room Captain served our table and the busboy received both the waiter's tip and his own.

Your New Best Friends

Let's assume that you find your tablemates convivial and your waitstaff ready, willing, and able to make your dining experience the best ever. There are still a couple of wrinkles that may need ironing. If half the table guests start standing in line ten minutes before the doors open and the other half linger over pre-dinner cocktails and show up ten minutes after, there could be a problem.

As a general rule, waiters are not going to start serving part of the table, particularly if it's a larger one, until all souls are present and accounted for. Or until the appointed door-closing moment, usually fifteen minutes after the scheduled seating.

They'll take orders, but they won't turn them in to the kitchen or serve.

Being first in the dining room gains you relatively little – the kitchen works on its own schedule. Do the experienced cruiser thing with your tablemates and suggest that everyone agrees to come to table five minutes late, maybe getting together for cocktails first.

People tend to come to the Main Dining Room for the first dinner *a la* Noah's Ark – two by two. And sit down two by two, partner with partner. And do the same thing for the whole cruise, including the same chairs. *Boring*. Take the lead on the first night and suggest changing seating arrangements with the dessert course. Experienced cruisers will often split up when they come to table, paving the way for others to do the same.

Another dicey area is the subject of wine at the table. It seems rude to order a bottle of wine – just for the two of you – and not share with the others, doesn't it? Stop! Would you offer the others a sip of your cocktail? Probably not. Keep that in mind. To make your position perfectly clear, you might ask, "Is anyone else ordering wine? What are you choosing? We're looking at that Cakebread Cellars Chardonnay."

Order from the Menu

Unless you're a serious foodie – and, maybe, even if you are – there are often menu items which are almost impossible to decode without a copy of *Larousse* at your side. Fortunately, most cruise lines offer a translation or the waiter can tell you that the *"entrêcote de boeuf aux champignons"* is steak with mushrooms. You always order from the menu in the Main Dining Room.

The dinner menu will be posted prominently just after lunch so you can start salivating.

Of Course

Breakfast is fairly straightforward. Juice and coffee appear immediately. You have the opportunity for more fruit (are Kadota figs served anywhere except on cruise ships?), eggs a number of ways, pancakes or waffles, potatoes, specialty dishes such as eggs benedict, and a variety of breakfast meats.

Lunch can easily stretch to four courses with an appetizer, soup or salad, entrée, and dessert. There's no requirement to choose something from each stanza of the menu at lunch.

At dinnertime, course work is the rule. First, an appetizer. Then soup. Then salad. Then your entrée. Then dessert. Five. At least. On Formal Nights, there may also be a sorbet course. Celebrity, generally considered tops for food among the mainstream cruise lines, offers five or six appetizers, three soups, two or more salads, and seven entrees each night at dinner. You won't find quite as many offerings on some other cruise lines, but you can count on a fish, a poultry, a beef, either a pork or a veal, and a pasta, whether as an appetizer or a main course. You can also count on a "spa" or "light and healthy" choice. The menu contains the chef's suggestions for the entire meal as well as the recommended low-cal, low-fat choices.

To the consternation of the international food specialists who plan shipboard cuisine, Americans' tastes aboard ship are not particularly adventurous. In the course of one interview, an executive chef vented. "Loawbster and steak. Steak and loawbster. And those %^@# shreemp coaktails."

In another interview, I took a highly-placed Celebrity official to task for removing my absolutely favorite appetizer, quail *paté*, from the menu. "But I loved it. I always had two servings."

"You and three other passengers, Madame." He went on, very smoothly, to assure me that I would adore the replacement, *mousseline of phay-zant*. Phay-zant? Oh. Pheasant. It was OK.

You heard it here first. A cruise is the time to eat adventurously. If you don't like something, send it back and order something else. If you do like it, you've just expanded your gustatory horizons.

Not Quite on the Menu

You need not be a slave to the menu. If you prefer a plain plate of boring iceberg lettuce rather than crunched-up romaine or hip, sexy mesclune, tell your waiter. You'll have it.

But be careful what you ask for – you'll keep getting it. And getting it. And getting it. Waiters take great pride in their memories for special requests. If you order iced tea or milk with dinner the first night out, it will appear, as reliably as sunset, at your place for the rest of the cruise unless you make it clear it was a one-time-only request. One request that never seems to sink in is milk, rather than cream, for coffee.

The more dedicated a cruise line is to family-oriented travel, the greater the variety of items on special children's menus. Think chicken fingers, pizza, spaghetti, burgers, and dogs. But the kids may surprise you by ordering from the regular menu and enjoying their choices.

Cruises are ideal venues for vegetarians. They find a far greater selection of meat-free meals than most regular restaurants offer. Folks who eschew (and don't chew) red meat will be in white meat heaven. Hard-line vegans probably should forego a diet of cruise food.

If you are on a special diet for a health condition – diabetes is the most common dietary concern – make your needs known to your travel agent when you book your cruise. And make sure the travel agent gets a response from the cruise line as to exactly how accommodating they will be. You may need to carry some of your own food items, such as salad dressings, jams and syrups, if they are important to you.

It is possible to keep kosher on a cruise ship. It may not be too interesting, but possible, it is. Kosher foods are usually boarded frozen, then thawed as the cruise progresses. Imagine a week of airline-type kosher meals. They probably come from the same kitchens. But you won't starve. *Shalom.*

Eat ... or Don't ... Without Guilt

Cruise ship waiters could teach the stereotypical Jewish mother something about guilt trips. If you dare to leave a morsel uneaten, the top-notch waiter assumes a look of confused dismay. "You did not like it?"

Hell, yes, I liked it, but I'm saving room for dessert. If you are not a plate-cleaner, make it clear to your waiter early on that you like to TASTE everything, just not EAT IT ALL. You will feel better and so will he.

If you really don't like something – the *Crème de Crappie* soup was over-salted and you didn't care for the garnish of toasted fins – roll your eyes at the waiter and, when he shimmers over, say, with regret, "I just don't care for this." It will be off the table and he will be on his way to the kitchen for a replacement (or not, as you wish) at the speed of a hopeful Olympian in training.

At the same time, if you are extraordinarily pleased by a particular dish, or just like to eat a lot, seconds are usually available. The kitchen staff probably does not understand the idea of simply putting one piece of meat on a small plate and handing it to the waiter. Most likely, you will get an entirely new plate of food.

Just because the courses march relentlessly on, you don't have to have soup for the soup course. You can have a second appetizer, served with the others' soups. It's possible to mix-and-match your dinner, just as long as whatever you want is on the menu. If it happens to be an evening when you fancy both the tiramisu and the crème brûlée for dessert, you can ask for a second salad instead of an entrée.

In The Alternative

You always have a choice as to your troughing venue for breakfast and lunch. The casual restaurant, usually a buffet, usually on the pool deck, caters to the hit-and-run crowd. The fare is steam-table predictable – particularly at breakfast. Scrambled eggs, pre-folded omelets, breakfast meats, semi-limp pancakes, fruits of all varieties (Kadota figs again!), dry cereals in their cunning little boxes, a hot cereal, yogurts, sweet rolls, bagels, and, usually, a meat and cheese platter. On some cruise lines, there is smoked salmon. And more smoked salmon. Hint: If the bridge crew is Norwegian, salmon is almost certain to show up.

Most ships also offer a custom-cooked egg station where a chef wields his omelet pans with cheese, chopped vegetables, and *elan*.

Come lunchtime, you may be taken by a hint of *déjà vu* when you notice that the salad dressings next to the green salad bar are the same ones served with dinner last night. There is always a green salad bar, followed by heartier salads based on pasta, rice, and potatoes. Plenty of deli-type meats and cheeses invite you to make a sandwich while, further down the line, the "made dishes" stay warm. If you jump to the conclusion that these are last night's leftovers, you're close. They're not really leftovers, they're "planned-overs". If the kitchen is going to roast 40 pork loins for dinner, why not roast 45 so there's pork to go into a sauce with Oriental vegetables. Very clever, these food people.

Almost at the end of the chow line, there's usually a carvery station with a roast of something or other. If you look around, you'll probably find a cousin of this morning's omelet chef whipping up the pasta dish of the day. Then, the final touch, desserts.

Before joining the feeding frenzy, walk the buffet line in the opposite direction from the traffic flow to see just what interests you. That way, you can leave room on your plate. And you can always go back.

Burgers, Dogs and 'Za

The fascination of American cruisers with pizza is a mystery. One of the most frequently asked questions on the Internet is, "What about the pizza?" To some people, 24-hour pizza is an important factor in choosing a cruise ship.

At lunchtime, a grill area fires up every day on every cruise ship unless it's raining pitchforks or a gale-force wind has blown up.

Burger and dogs, dogs and burgers. The standard condiments are available for your Cheeseburger in Paradise and, um, did you want fries with that? It's not a highly creative lunch but if you don't feel like shuffling down a buffet line or just don't want to put on shoes, it's an option. Do not expect to ask for your burger rare. It's not allowed, due to health regulations. Do expect, under these circumstances, that your burger will be a bit dry, if not a suitable substitute for pressed sawdust on a roll.

The Buffet By Night

Some ships, particularly the mega-type with over 2,000 passengers, turn the casual restaurant into something a bit more upscale when the sun goes down. Generally, it's open seating so you can eat when you wish, the dress code is casual, and the appetizers, soups and entrees are the same as those served in the Main Dining Room. The main difference is in the serving. Usually you serve yourself, buffet-style, everything but the entrée, which you order from the menu. The waiters will tell you what to do.

This is not an option on all ships. If it's important to you – if you refuse to dress up for a formal night, for example – make sure you check the availability in advance.

Wonderland by Night

Not all evening transformations are equal. In the year before this book was written, we tried a number of different evening alternatives and are hard-pressed to choose which we liked best. On *Marco Polo,* we savored an Oriental dinner – complete with endless saki – and an evening of French cuisine with great wine choices included. On *Norwegian Dream,* we were regulars at the line's signature alternative restaurant, Le Bistro. On *Diamond* we paid two visits to the high-energy Don Vito's Trattoria, repeating a similar experience from the year before on Radisson fleetmate *Song of Flower.*

Try as we might, we can't find any commonalties among these experiences except the small number of diners served with the corollary increase in quality and personal attention. Practically, the Main Dining Room usually does a fantastic job of serving upscale banquet food. The alternative restaurants are closer in ambience and quality to a landside restaurant.

Expect a small service charge for this sort of alternate dining.

Room Service – Day or Night

Most cruisers don't explore room service any further than hanging their "coffee and" orders on the door before retiring for the night. The room service menu is in the nicely bound folder outlining the ship's services. The fare is usually simple – sandwiches, salads, and desserts – but a fruit and cheese plate can be just the thing to tide you over before dinner. And a couple of sandwiches fit nicely in The Giant Tote Bag for a picnic ashore.

Room service is, almost always, without charge except for alcoholic beverages and canned soda. Toss one of those dollar bills hiding in The Container to the person who delivers your order.

If you leave the mainstream fleet for the smaller, more upscale liners, or have a top suite, you can order from the Main Dining Room menu and have dinner served *en suite* or on your private balcony if you wish.

Yo, Ho, Ho and a Bottle of Rum (or Vodka, or Scotch ...)

Alcoholic beverages by the drink are expensive, on land or at sea. If you do indulge, it's not unlikely you'll be a little more likely to do so on a cruise vacation. After all, you're not driving.

Belly Up to the Bar

Liquor is a profit center for ships just as it is for landside restaurants. And, with the notable exception of one mainstream cruise line, a standard 15% gratuity is added to every bar order, includ-

ing soft drinks by the can everywhere and wine by the bottle in the dining rooms. This adds up rather quickly if you enjoy anything more than a single Martini before dinner. What adds up even more quickly is the kids and their soda pop.

B.Y.O.B. – Pops

There are people who like beer. There are people who like a lot of beer, especially in hot weather. "Hops pops" at $3 or more per can, plus 15%, get pricey as do soda pops at almost as much. I don't recommend you try to cart three or four cases of your favorite brewskis on board with a hand truck, but there are ways to self-supply. Buy enough cheap suitcases to hold your provisions. Cushion the contents with bubble wrap, top, bottom, and sides. Check the bags, do not attempt to carry them on.

Beer and sodas are rather disgusting when warm, so your cabin steward must be enlisted. It's his job to figure out how to keep your supply cold. A discreet offering of "salad" will increase his interest in assisting. Once the beer is cold, make sure he knows that he's welcome to help himself.

An extremely efficient cooler can be constructed from everyday shopping bags lined with plastic trash bags. Fill with beer (or sodas) and add ice. Don't try this anywhere but in your cabin's shower. Remove your "cooler" before using the shower for its intended purpose. Don't forget foam can "cozies".

B.Y.O.B. – Wine & Spirits

There's no hard-and-fast rule about bringing your own aboard. Each cruise line has its own policy. The policies range from, "If we find you bringing it on board, we'll confiscate it and give it back at the end of the cruise," to the far more liberal, "Please do not consume personal beverages in public areas."

To further confuse things, some lines allow you to purchase spirits in their duty-free shops for immediate, on-board consumption while others won't deliver your purchases until the last night out. This is definitely a "go figure" situation. Or, perhaps better, a "go find out" challenge.

As in many other things, discretion is the better part of valor. But why do you think almost every cabin features an ice bucket, glasses, and cocktail napkins? Obviously, there's some sort of expectation that you might be carrying your own supply.

We've never had a problem with tucking bottles into our suitcases, using clothes as breakage buffers. If you're truly paranoid, wrap each bottle in bubble wrap and seal inside a plastic bag.

Just breakfast, lunch, and dinner? What about the Midnight Buffet?

There's almost always food to be found somewhere on a cruise ship. Coffee and tea usually appear on a weather deck or in the casual restaurant at 6 AM. Breakfast, or some form of it, is usually served until almost lunchtime. Casual lunch usually folds up in mid-afternoon, not long before teatime which, in turn, isn't long before the first dinner seating. Some ships feature "happy hours" with appropriate snack foods – but the drinks aren't two for one.

If you're the late seating sort (we are), a saunter by the late afternoon tea buffet yields delicacies that hit the spot with an in-cabin cocktail. A plate of little sandwiches, a plate of sweets, maybe fruit and cheese – whatever looks good. The rules usually say not to take food to cabins. This makes no sense because room service brings food to cabins all the time. There are no food police to stop you.

The every-night midnight buffet is almost a thing of the past in these calorie- and fat-conscious days. Instead, hot snacks are often passed in the public rooms starting around 11PM. There will be at least one big-deal midnight buffet – usually on the second formal night. Be prepared for a huge crush of people, all pushing to get to the food first. Most cruise lines offer a fifteen-minute grace period for folks who wish to photograph the opulence.

If this isn't enough food, there's always room service – on some cruise lines it operates 24 hours a day – complete with 24-hour pizza.

Why do you prefer the late seating to the main seating?

Basically, it gives us a longer day and we're accustomed to eating on the late side at home. We also enjoy the time to relax before dinner after a day in port. If your stomach (or your kids') starts getting peckish in late afternoon, you're probably better off with main seating. Be warned, however, that main seating breakfasts come awfully early!

I don't think we could bring enough sodas to keep our kids supplied. What to do without breaking the budget?

There are almost always "free" beverages available – usually iced tea, lemonade and fruit punch. Soda by the glass is usually included at dinner. Some enlightened cruise lines sell soda cards for unlimited pop.

We've heard that cruise ship coffee is pretty awful. We are coffee snobs. Any ideas?

Of course. Remember, coffee for huge numbers of people is "institutional" at best and just brewed will taste a lot better than "bottom of the pot". The one cruise line that had a reputation for perfectly terrible coffee finally found the problem and cured it.

There are two choices. Bring along individual coffee bags and order tea from room service and in the restaurants. Don't try to order hot water, it will only confuse the crew. The second choice is to pack a small, four-cup coffee maker in your Creature Comfort Bag and bring along your own special blend. Don't forget the filters. You will probably need an extension cord unless you fancy making coffee in the head during morning ablutions. Approach #2 does not work well in dining rooms.

I'm really worried about gaining ten pounds. All that food!

Just because it's there doesn't mean you have to eat it. In fact, with such an array of choices, you can balance your calories throughout the day and really enjoy two desserts.

What if we don't finish our bottle of wine at dinner? May we take it to our cabin?

Probably. Otherwise, your waiter will put it back in the cellar for you and bring it out at your request. The storage method is ideal if one person enjoys wine and the traveling partner abstains.

We'd like to bring our own special wines along. Is that permitted? How does it work in the dining room?

This depends, largely, on the cruise line's policy. And there's always the delicious possibility that your travel agent or a friend will send a *Bon Voyage* bottle. Usually, personal wines are subject to a corkage fee, somewhere in the $5-$10 range.

On one or two cruises, we've been in gift wine overload. A crisp $20 to the sommelier first night out took care of the corkage charges. We tipped another $10 at voyage's end.

Can we buy liquor in port and bring it on board?

Sure, if you're willing to pay local prices and be discreet as you carry it on. In some ports, if you purchase duty free liquor, it will be delivered directly to the ship and held in bond until the last night out when it is delivered to your cabin. In others, if you can schlep it away from the store, it's yours. Two popular ports, Bermuda and St. Thomas, take opposite tactics. Bermuda delivers to the ship. In St. Thomas, you can schlep.

Do cruise lines ever charge "extra" for food?

Some extract an extra charge for upscale ice cream bars, designer coffees, etc. And if you hit the caviar bar, you'll get hit.

What about special occasions? We're taking a cruise for a big birthday.

Your travel agent can make all the necessary arrangements for a cake to appear at your table, accompanied by a rather off-key rendition of the birthday song. (Same deal for anniversaries.) It's a good idea to check with the maitre d' to ensure that your wishes will be fulfilled.

GODIVA

COOKIES

Good Stuff
Boutique

HOLIDAY
CRUISE

PER
FUME

CHAPTER SIX

CONSPICUOUS CONSUMPTION

In this chapter, we'll look at one of the ways you can part with money – and how to deal with money – on your all-inclusive cruise vacation. Other than tipping, there are two basic methods: shopping and gambling.

Shopping definitely comes first.

Money Changers in the Temple

A great American philosopher, Jimmy Buffett, once said that there are two kinds of Americans who leave our shores – tourists and travelers. A tourist wants to take America along on a trip. The traveler wants to experience something a bit different. What could be more American than pictures of dead presidents (and Ben Franklin plus, if you're really flush, Salmon P. Chase) in your wallet or purse?

If your destination is Totally Tourist (think the Caribbean or Mexican Riviera), you don't need to take anyone with you except George (for tips), Abe, Alex, Andy, Ben, and company. When you reach ports where tourism isn't the #1 pastime, you may need to exchange your images for those honored by your host country.

High on the totally strange list, I was able to purchase a beautiful linen dress in Tallin, Estonia for $40 US. My husband, bored by waiting around for me, could not purchase a Coke at the McDonald's across the square because he didn't have any local currency.

The ship's staff will happily exchange your U$ for local currency. The reason they are happy is because the cruise line collects a fee for the service. They become even happier when you pay another service fee to put whatever you didn't spend back into U$ before they become ecstatic changing your new U$ into the coin of the next realm.

Everyone's idea of walking-around money is different. We generally carry the equivalent of $100 per person, per day, with a $100 bill tucked deep into wallet or pocketbook in case of true emergency.

You'll probably use a credit card for major purchases but what about that Coke at McDonald's? So far, the only place we've visited that doesn't have McDonald's restaurants is Viet Nam and we've never found a McDonald's outside the Caribbean that doesn't require local currency unless the local dollar is on a par with the U.S. dollar. If you'll be taking public transportation, you'll have to pay in local legal tender.

The more "foreign" your port, and the further you go from tourist-related sites, the more likely you are to need local currency.

We once made a significant miscalculation on walking-around money. We were in St. Petersburg, Russia, freelancing. Blissed out after several hours in the Hermitage (we paid the entry fees by credit card) we crossed the street and boarded the fast boat to Peterhof – 80 rubles each which pretty much tapped us out. At the entry kiosk for the summer palace, the martinet selling tickets wanted nothing to do with our U$ or our credit cards. A nice British couple kindly offered to sell us the entry fee. A bus from another cruise line offered final salvation – we hitched a ride back to the pier with their official excursion group.

The best exchange rates, bar none, are found at American Express offices. There is precious little time in many ports and the ship's trip probably won't include a stop at an AmEx outpost. You may be better off biting the bullet and changing your money aboard ship. The truly thrifty can organize a cartel – maybe among their tablemates – and pay a single fee for changing several people's bucks and spreading the cost around. This assumes a flat fee regardless of the amount.

Some countries feature curb-side money exchange machines. Insert your $20 U.S. and get the equivalent in local currency – less a service charge and a not so

favorable exchange rate. Your $20 may result in the equivalent of fifteen dollars in kroner.

Don't Leave Home Without It

Actually, don't leave home without two different credit cards each – preferably paid-off cards. You don't want to become the Purser's dance partner on debarkation day because you've maxed out a card with purchases ashore and Mr. Credit Card Company just says, "NO!"

Why two? And why two different ones? Each? If a pocket is picked or a purse stolen, you want to cancel the cards immediately. The Purser's office is extremely helpful in such situations. You're probably not going to stop shopping, and you have to settle your on-board account, so the second person's cards come into play. If your traveling companion is not your spouse, each person should carry one of the other person's cards for a belt-and-suspenders level of security.

If you are traveling solo, have two sets of two. Two with you and two in the safe.

Credit card companies don't like to lose money when a card is stolen and huge balances are run up. The cardholder's liability is usually only $50. Accounts with unusual activity – particularly unusual activity in a different area code – attract the attention of security folks. If security gets a heads-up about unusual activity, someone will call you to make sure you're the one who's been using the card. If you're on a cruise, you won't be answering the phone. The card company just might cancel the card and you'll be in for a rude surprise when you step up to the cashier to settle your purchases.

For peace of mind, call your credit card companies and advise them that you will be traveling and making charges. And while you're at it, write down the international phone number for reporting a lost or stolen card.

El Shoppiando

That's a "Spanglish" term I invented to describe one of my favorite activities when I lived in San Juan and shopped my way through the Caribbean in the early '70s. People who rarely or never engage in *el shoppiando* at home do so, with a vengeance, on vacations, cruises included. It may just be T-shirts for the kids and grandkids or it may be high-end jewelry, electronics, or cameras.

Shopping falls into two classes – bargains and souvenirs. If one purchase can be both, you win. It's *trés cool* to have a guest admire a *tchotke* and be able to answer, airily, "Oh, I found that in the greatest little shop in Cartagena. Only three dollars."

Folk arts and crafts are great souvenirs. Just make sure the piece is indigenous to the country. It's no fun to give a friend a little carved cat from your Caribbean vacation and notice, as she unwraps it, a sticker that says, "Made in China."

The more touristy your destination, the less likely you are to grab a bargain.

Duty Free?

Back in 1993, I coined a phrase, to my husband's dismay, "It is my duty to shop; I assure you it will not be free." All mainstream cruise lines feature duty-free shops on board. That doesn't mean you won't have to pay import duties, a nice way of saying taxes, when you return to the U.S. on the amount you spent – aboard ship or ashore – if it exceeds the amount designated by U.S. Customs. The oral tradition has it that your on-board purchases will be reported if they exceed a certain limit. Other unsubstantiated rumors include port vendors reporting large purchases.

Some ports, St. Thomas is the one that comes immediately to mind for most people, are touted as "duty free." To be sure, vice-related products (liquor and tobacco) are much cheaper than your own home port. But there hasn't been a true bargain in St. Thomas since Gerald Ford was President. I know. I keep looking. Recently, a Bottega Venetta bag was $20 more on St. Thomas than in New York.

If you want to cheat and buy more than your allowance of hooch, you probably won't get caught. But it's a lot easier to stock up on the pricey stuff such as liqueurs and cordials and pay the duty. It's still less expensive than your local *vin marchand's* prices. If you can find a hometown purveyor of spirits who issues a catalog, take one along. Then you'll know for sure that $15 for the artichoke brandy is a good deal.

Best Bargain Buys the World Around

Bargains can usually be found in a product's country of origin. Easy to understand. No shipping, no export/import costs. And there's the benefit of a refund of the VAT (Value Added Tax) in many European countries. But before you spring, think how your bargain is going to find its way home.

Almost anything is worth what you're willing to pay for it. That said, here are some of the best bargains/souvenirs we've found in six of the seven continents. (We understand that penguins are not for sale in Antarctica, but we haven't tried to buy one. Yet.)

Mexico – Silver jewelry. It should be stamped .926 (which may or may not mean that it is) and should be hand-created, not machined. The best pieces come from Taxco. Know the going per-ounce price of silver. If you have the opportunity, Tlaquepaque, a suburb of Guadalajara, is a bargain shopper's heaven for craftwork.

Hong Kong – Almost anything at Stanley Market. Jade at the Jade Market. Pearls.

Tourists are rare at the Jade Market; don't go there unless you know what you're doing. If you do, it's worth it. My singular sensation purchase was an elaborately carved three-colored piece, which I wear as a pendant, for 70 U$. After three hours of shopping and bargaining. Appraised value back at home – $2,000.

London– China. Best place, the Reject China Shop on Regent Street. You don't even have to go there. You can e-mail your order. Harrod's logo goods are great souvenirs and gifts. Tea from

Fortnum & Mason. Don't think about buying a Burberry's raincoat. They're cheaper in the U.S.

Oslo, Norway – Dale's Sweaters. About half of what you might pay in the U.S. Best place, the Oslo Sweater Shops – one at the pier, the other downtown. If you find a sweater you like but your size isn't available, have the clerk call the other shop. Charge everything on one chit. Better VAT refund.

A sweater I admired was available in a ship's shop for $179. I bought the same sweater at OSS for $110 and received a VAT refund.

Copenhagen, Denmark – Royal Copenhagen china. Visit their shop on the Strøget – a Traveler's Rest with clean restrooms, free sodas and U.S. newspapers. The downstairs display of Flora Danica is beyond belief. But you can't buy it all. Their "seconds" shop is upstairs.

Mallorca – Pearls. Pearls. Pearls. They're not the "real" pearls you can buy in other countries, but they look great. Especially the black ones.

Australia – Paddy's Market in Sydney for souvenir goods. Everything that's for sale in the pricey little shops downtown, you can buy at Paddy's for about one third the price. Coogi sweaters at about one-half of U.S. prices are everywhere. Don't miss the Queen Victoria Building – possibly the most elegant mall in the world.

Costa Rica and Colombia – Coffee. Don't buy it at a dockside store, go to a local market. ("*¿Dondé está el mercado de comidas mas cerca?*") At home, keep it in the freezer for freshness.

San Blas Islands – Molas. Don't expect to bargain. A $10 mola on the shopping island is the same thing that sells for $40 or more elsewhere.

Alaska – For T-shirts, sweatshirts, and other gimcracks, the Skagway Outlet Store – SOS – at the end of the main street in Skagway.

Puerto Rico – Rum. Don Q. Feel like a felon scoring 1.75 liter bottles at the *muelle* (pier) duty-free shops. You can bring back all you're able to carry or are willing to trust to baggage handlers. There is no limit to the amount of rum you can bring to the Mainland.

Stockholm, Sweden – This may be an aberration, but we scored two dozen Kosta-Boda candleholders for the equivalent of $7 US each. Same candleholders in Copenhagen, $15 US. In the U.S. they are $35.

We've experienced plenty of non-bargains, too. And not every port has a best bargain. As a rule, the closer any outlet is to the pier, the higher the price seems to be.

When a Bargain Isn't

The #1 rule for offshore shopping is to know what the same thing would cost at home. This applies to jewelry, probably more than anything else. If you're buying machined gold jewelry, ask to have it weighed and know the going rate. Semi-precious colored stones – tanzanite, aquamarine, garnet, topaz, kunzite, etc., are popular and often overpriced souvenir purchases. Know what a chunk of your stone of choice costs then add (generously) $100 for the mounting and see if the dealer is in the ballpark. Don't get too excited if there are diamonds in the setting. Small diamonds cost almost more to mount than to buy. I don't recommend purchasing the "Big Three and P" (Sapphires, Rubies, and Emeralds plus Pearls – to say nothing of Diamonds) anywhere but from a trusted jeweler stateside, unless you know what you're doing and your loupe is next to your credit cards. For jewelry, or any other significant purchase, use a credit card. If it turns out to be a good fake or appraises significantly lower than the purchase price, start screeching.

The people at the ubiquitous emerald stores will argue with me, but the most prized emeralds are not bright green, nor are the best sapphires navy blue.

Important stones should come with a certificate of authenticity.

Make sure you're shopping for apples, not oranges, particularly with cameras, binoculars and electronics. Find a *Sunday New York Times* and rip out the 47th Street Photo ad. There's your standard of comparison. Last year's items are not a bargain.

Most of the time you will get a list of "preferred" stores in your daily ship's daily newspaper. Often the ship guarantees the quality of the merchandise at one of their preferred merchants. After all, you may never visit this island again, and the merchants are well aware of that. But if you're looking for a bargain, you probably won't get the best price in one of the recommended stores.

Bargain Basement?

How to know when to bargain, when not? If you hadn't skipped the port lecture for the next stop, the Cruise Director probably would have told you the local customs. Ask the person sitting next to you on the deck.

When you ask a vendor, "How much?" and, in response to the first offer, you display your best look of confusion and minor disbelief and the price drops, he or she is open for bargaining. (This can be practiced at your bathroom mirror at home or aboard ship with a willing partner.)

If the "look" didn't do it, have your shopping partner say, "There was one like it for a lot less at that store around the corner." A response from the shopkeeper of, "Then buy it there!" definitely closes the bargaining door. The only way to save face in this scenario is for you to look at the shopping partner and announce, stoutly, "But I like this one better."

There's an unwritten law in some of the countries where bargaining rules that the beginning of negotiations means that a sale will take place. In other countries, walking away is just part of the game. The more expensive the item, the more important it is to be aware of local customs. If you waste a shopkeeper's time – particularly if you have accepted hospitality from him such as a cup of tea or a cold drink – and don't buy? Your name will be mud in that port before you're ever out of his establishment. There will be no bargains that day anywhere. Think cellphones, from Tijuana to Istanbul.

The Moscow Theory of Shopping

Credit for inventing this term and *modus operandi* belongs to one of my personal icons, Suzy Gershman, author of the *Born to Shop* series of books. *Born To Shop*, together with a *Lonely Planet* guide, is all I need to know about a new city to get ready for adventure and *el shoppiando*.

The Moscow Theory is a simple one. See it, want it, buy it. You have to really want it for the theory to kick in. It's your time you're wasting if you decide to cruise around to other stores to score a lower price. If you can even find the same thing.

There is nothing worse to a confirmed practitioner of el shoppiando *than going back to buy whatever it was that you were comparison shopping only to discover that the store is closed for siesta and your ship's about to leave or that what you lusted after was just sold. Probably to the person at the next table. I still mourn a beautiful silver necklace (shop closed) on Cozumel and a fabulous dress (sold) in Puerto Vallarta.*

Sometimes the bargain finds you. I really didn't want those two sets of nesting baskets in Hanoi. How was I going to get them home? I just kept saying, "No." And I meant it. Finally, they were only $2, down from $10. I bought them.

The Moscow Theory applies particularly to cruisers on official shore excursions. You don't get much chance to shop around. Escaping from the tour group to shop on your own is seriously frowned upon in some of the more up-tight countries.

It's The Custom

As you return from your vacation to the land of the free and the home of the brave, you'll be asked to tell Uncle Sam, wearing his Customs Official outfit, just what you purchased when you were out of the country and how much you paid for it. It's not nice to fool either Mother Nature or Uncle Sam. But people do it, some more successfully than others.

In the process of interviewing a Customs inspector at Kennedy Airport in New York, I learned the most fascinating – and backward – rule of all. If the person looks comfortably well-off and professes to have spent very little, a big red flag starts waving. Even if you really didn't spend anything (and we really didn't on a recent Caribbean cruise) say you did or you may have uniformed folks looking through your lingerie.

The same man also shared some of the best-known dodges. Interestingly, they all involved jewelry and cameras and the compulsion of the would-be tricksters to display them in the open.

•Pearls from the Far East. So perfect they almost look fake except to the trained eye. Strung quickly with shoddy knots and closed with a cheap clasp. Gotcha!

•Rings or bracelets that would put a family of four over the limit in one fell swoop. The jewelry looks filthy from intense applications of SOS pads without rinsing afterward. Gotcha!

•And the cameras. The latest, most expensive models with many fancy lenses. They look like they lost a blood feud fight with a riding lawnmower. Gotcha!

•The Burberry raincoat I told you not to buy? Still snappy with sizing but stained on the seat and cuffs. And you probably have the VAT refund slip in your wallet or purse. Gotcha!

If you're over your limit by a few dollars, fudging may be tolerated depending upon your own moral standards. If you're w-a-y over, declare your stuff and haul out your credit card. After all, there are states whose sales taxes are almost equal to or greater than the Customs duty. The U.S. Government's computers are massive and mighty. If you get caught trying to gouge a few bucks in the Customs line, don't you think the IRS is going to take a very close look at your next 1040?

What about travelers' checks? Good idea?

To some extent, travelers' checks (or cheques) are a holdover from the days before universal acceptance of credit cards and an ATM on every corner.

Travelers' checks have a high aggravation factor on cruise vacations. It takes time to buy them and time to change them into cash. Even if they're free, that's relative. Local currency on cruise ships is the American dollar. Change your travelers' checks, then you get to pay the fee to change the U.S. dollars into the local currency where you're getting off the ship.

Assuming you don't get taken out by *banditos* on the way to the cruise ship, carrying sufficient folding money is the easiest way to go. Once you board, your cash – except what you decide is indicated for an individual day, is in the safe along with your gambling and tip money – ready to go for the next day.

Underwear offers a dandy way to stash cash. Ladies can put bills inside their bras (Wonder® or otherwise) and lots of the silk boxers sold these days feature condom pockets where folded bills may be carefully stored.

What if I run out of money?

That depends upon your definition of "run out." If you're out of cash, the casino cashier's cage will be happy to give you greenbacks for a fairly hefty charge against your credit card. Some cruise ships feature ATM machines. At least in our experience, by the time people want to "tap the MAC", MAC's been tapped out. I have yet to see a helicopter fly in to reload an ATM machine.

If you run out of money in port, ATMs are almost everywhere. Some, however, require an international PIN. Make sure you know before you go.

Growing up, I never really understood the term "mad money" – but my mom always made sure I had some. I thought it was there for spending on something silly – not for finding my way home in time of crisis. Read that: I got mad at my date. Even though I'm an even-tempered person, I always travel with mad money. A crisp U.S. $100 or two, tucked behind my photo ID. My husband does the same. (Remember those fast boats from Bermuda that can catch up to a departing cruise ship?)

Can't I just write a check?

It's a good idea to have a check or two with you, but cash and credit cards rule travelers' commerce.

What if we have a pre-cruise hotel overseas? Where do we change our money?

If you arrive at your destination airport during regular hours, there will be a change booth open and more than willing to zap you with a serious surcharge for changing your dollars.

If you're saving money with overnight flights, arranging your own transport to the hotel, or traveling on holidays (not ours, the holidays there) you may be out of luck. The best deal is what personal service bankers call "tip packs." They are usually available in multiples of $20 U.S. currency, changed into the pesos, drachmas, or rubles of your destination country. Ask for them ahead of time – two or more weeks. The exchange rate is favorable and if you're a good customer of the bank, the transaction may be made without charge.

Once in your pre- (or post-) cruise country's hotel, the hotel's front desk is the most convenient place for exchanges but the rake-off is high. You have to decide whether saving a dollar or two is worth the aggravation. Banks and American Express offices are always the best – but factor in the time you will lose standing in line.

Things to Buy

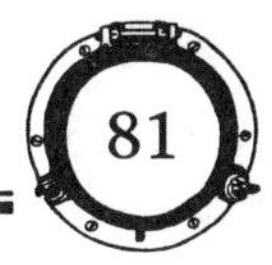

TAKING A CHANCE

Craps float. So do blackjack, roulette, weird forms of poker (including video), and the ubiquitous slots. Cruising and casinos are almost synonymous. Then you've got your bingo, your poolside horseracing, and your standard mileage pool. Opportunities to contribute to one of every cruise line's most important profit centers are almost everywhere.

At one time or another my husband and I have played all these games, with varying degrees of success. He can usually be counted on to win at least the tip money by posing as a $5 James Bond at the blackjack tables. I reliably lose my stake to the slots with the stunning exception of hitting a $250 jackpot on *Marco Polo* the last night out as we steamed toward Sydney from Melbourne.

Did I say "last night out"? You bet. Right Now is the moment when you learn the real truth about shipboard slots. Make yourself an umbrella drink. Be seated.

Tab "A" In Slot "B"

Everybody – and that's everybody – knows and believes as gospel, that slots are "looser" the first part of a cruise and "tighter" as the cruise goes on. Everybody also knows that this is so passengers, made greedy by tales of big hits the first or second night out, will pour ever-increasing numbers of quarters into the bandits in hopes of hitting, too. Right? Experienced cruisers, who know the real truth make their offerings to the gods of chance the first and second nights and stay away for the rest of the cruise. Right?

Wrong-O.

Did you ever stop to think just how such a thing could happen? Captain Stubing and Gopher creeping around in the dark of night with a device that looks like a roller skate key? Not likely.

Did you know that today's slots are nothing more (or less) than computers? Just like your personal computer, your personal slot machine has a chip called an EPROM – that means Electronically Programmable Read Only Memory. Read Only. That means that nobody, but nobody, can change what that chip tells the slot machine/computer without a whole lot of trouble. The entire computer (slot machine) has to be opened, one EPROM removed and another put in its place.

Each machine is set to the cruise line's payout percentage when it leaves the factory. It doesn't change. The cruise line can set the real jackpot, the one your chances of winning are about a bazillion to one. Standard jackpots are 10,000 coins or 25,000 coins. The worst news? Those reels with 7's and apples and cherries and whatever? Not real. Just there for the show. The computer already knows whether or not you've won.

Slot machines offer the worst odds of winning of any form of gambling short of a state lottery. The bells and lights combine with the distinctive "clank" of coins hitting the metal tray to give the customer a sense that somewhere, someone is getting rich. The next one could be you. Statistics say it won't be.

Now that we've debunked that seagoing legend, what about the experience we've all had? After pumping $20 in quarters into a machine, we walk away in disgust. A sweet little old lady wearing a powder blue dress and sensible shoes drops in a few quarters and all the bells and whistles go off, stopping us in our tracks. Granny hit the jackpot. If only we'd pulled the handle one more time. Give it up; it makes no difference at all.

New sets of numbers are constantly being generated in a random fashion by the machine's infernal internal computer. Your "hit" is determined by the exact second (or, more likely, nanosecond) you push the button or pull the handle, not by the number of cumulative "plays" on that machine.

We don't need anyone to teach us how to pull the handle or push the button. The other games afloat are a bit more challenging to the novice.

Over 21

If a ship has only one "table game", it's blackjack. The concept is simple. Whoever, you or the dealer, is closer to 21 without going over, wins. Arguably, blackjack (and its wealthy cousin baccarat) is the only casino game where intelligence, experience and skill come into play. Entire books have been written on How To Win At Blackjack and there are several outstanding computer games to help you learn the necessary skills. Most cruise lines provide gaming guides for passengers and the casino staff is happy to teach you the ins and outs of table games during an at-sea day – before you hit the tables in the evening.

Blackjack is the only casino game where one can improve the odds with a little skill. You can learn basic blackjack strategy in a short time from one of the many books on the subject. If you know what you are doing, the odds favor the house less, and you more, than any other casino game.

Just as each table has a minimum (the least expensive tend to be $3 or $5), it has a maximum. There's a good reason for this. Anyone with a passing knowledge of statistics knows that, sooner or later, you're going to win. So, if you double your bet each time you lose, you'll at least stay even when the winning hand appears. Doubling losses works only five times at blackjack tables. If you lose the sixth hand, you're done.

High Rollers?

The term "high roller" came, originally, from the craps tables but these days it means anyone with a significant amount of money to gamble. True high rollers are rare on cruise ships; they don't like to consort with the amateurs. "Medium rollers" are more frequently observed. Probably only the casino staff will know who the rollers are – they come aboard with letters of credit from land-based casinos. A $20,000 letter of credit is medium. $50,000 is high.

Most of us won't share table space with serious players but if one happens along, there's a dramatic change in the aura surrounding the table. The dealer, cheerful and helpful to the honeymoon couple at the end of the table up 'til now, turns serious. Your $5 ante suddenly looks paltry compared to the fellow with the diamond pinky ring playing two hands at $50 or $100 each. Remember, you' re playing against the dealer just as the roller is. Concentrate.

Wheel of Fortune?

Roulette may be the most benign casino game ever invented. With any luck at all, placing only the most conservative bets, you can while away two or three hours at the wheel of fortune without winning much or losing everything. There are two 50:50 bets available – red or black, odd or even. After that, the odds escalate in favor of the house.

The even money bets really aren't 50:50. The wheel has 38 spaces but only 36 of them are red/black or odd/even. The 0 and 00 spaces are what give the house the advantage. An even money bet will win 9 times out of 19 giving the house about a 5% advantage.

A Bunch of ????

Craps is fast-paced and, at best, confusing to the uninitiated. This may be why the house enjoys the least advantage of any game. In simplest terms, when a "new shooter" comes out, he or she rolls the dice to determine the "point" that must be made on a subsequent roll. If the shooter rolls a 7 or an 11, it's an instant winner. Roll a 2, 3, or 12, and it's an instant loser. Any other roll (4, 5, 6, 8, 9 or 10) becomes the "point". Now the shooter has to roll the point before rolling a 7. Everyone else pressing around the table bets on the likelihood of the shooter winning, or not winning. And much, much more. You're on your own putting chips down where you think you want them to be; there's no middleman in craps. The only way most people can tell how they're doing at craps is watching the croupier deal with their stack of chips. If he takes them away, you lost. If he shoves another stack over, you won.

Calculating the odds on the various combinations of play in craps is an exercise for a Ph.D. thesis in statistics. You have your best chance when you play the "pass" line with odds. The worst odds are the "hard way" or any of the other boxes in the center of the table. But craps is the most interactive of the table games. You and the others around the table can have a lot of fun while you lose your money.

Weird Poker Games

Nowhere else are the odds more in favor of the house (cruise line) than in the ever-proliferating forms of stud poker. This isn't sitting around, drinking a beer, smoking a cigar, bluffing your buddies, poker. It's serious (and expensive) business. You – and everyone else at the table – are playing against the dealer. The rules are bizarre and vary from cruise line to cruise line, game to game. If it's called "Caribbean Stud", the progression of winnings is a formula owned by a Florida company called Progressive Games. They receive a royalty on every table where the game is played. Other lines give remarkably similar games different names and don't pay the royalties. If you happen to win, it's a big win. Otherwise, it's the ocean-going version of pouring money down a rat hole. "Let it Ride" is a fascinating method of extracting even more money from players under the guise of, "Hey, this is so easy even I can play it."

Just for Fun ... and a Few Bucks

The non-casino games – Jackpot Bingo, pool deck horseracing, and the mileage pool – are, say casino managers, for entertainment only. Arguably, it's easy to be entertained by winning a few thousand dollars playing Jackpot Bingo on the final night of the cruise. Again, it's pure chance. The one place where you think you might be able to score is the mileage pool. If you're contemplating taking a laptop computer and a GPS system, forget it. My husband and one of his buddies tried it. They knew, within seven feet, exactly where in the middle of the ocean we were and, through a few quick mathematical calculations, knew exactly how far the ship had traveled. They put some serious money into the pool as did the bikini-clad babes watching the distinguished looking gentlemen figure it out. Did they win? No. That night at dinner, I braced the Master of the Vessel about this problem. "Ah. Madame. Somebody on the bridge makes up the number. It is usually close."

Casino Royale

Our gambling experiences range from the two blackjack tables and seven slot machines aboard Radisson's *Song of Flower* to the mega-ships where you'd swear you were in Atlantic City if the deck wasn't rolling. Until the *Grand Princess* came down the ways, the largest casino afloat was on Carnival's *Destiny,* but there are more to come. The biggest payout, a record still in place after more than four years, was on Carnival's *Jubilee,* $1,065,428.22. How can this be? The Carnival/Holland America fleet plays a progressive jackpot where the bets from each of 11 ships are linked. There's no limit to the size of the jackpot. A warning: MegaCash isn't available fleet-wide. Check to make sure if it's that important to you.

Atlantic City or Atlantic Ocean?

One of the big differences between casinos afloat and those ashore is the attitude of the dealers, croupiers, and other casino employees. Years back, on-board casinos were usually concessions. Today, most cruise lines staff the casinos with their own employees. Dealers and croupiers ashore (to say nothing of pit bosses that remind us of pit bulls) are not always the heart and soul of charm. Instead, they're all business. Big business. At sea, the casino employees are as important to the cruise experience as the cruise director, the purser's staff, or anyone else whom passengers meet along the way. The difference? On land, the destination is a casino or casinos with the express purpose of the

trip being GAMBLING. On a cruise ship, gambling is just one of many entertainments.

According to David Stanley, RCI's Vice President for casino operations, "Casinos have to match other customer services and facilities, then try just a little bit harder. Everything else aboard is free!"

A few truths about gambling at sea; most learned the hard way

- You'll almost always walk through the casino on your way to wherever it is you want to go. This is called marketing.
- Once you're aboard the ship, separate the cash you'll need for tips on the final night, put it in an envelope, and stash it in the safe.
- Know what you can afford to lose and chalk it up to "entertainment." The biggest mistake you can make is pouring your (rare) winnings straight back into the casino's coffers. Wouldn't you rather have that Coogi sweater from Australia, a Lalique figurine, or a Colombian emerald instead of another few minutes at a table or a machine?
- The fastest and best way to rid yourself of your gambling stake is seating yourself in front of a video poker or blackjack machine. This won't hurt, did it?
- Always, always, always wash your hands when you leave the casino. There's a reason for calling it "filthy lucre". It is. This is especially true for those who play the slots and handle coinage rather than chips.
- Know that every time you hit your sail-and-spend card for the max ($1,000 per day on most cruise lines) you're probably going to be looking at that bill for a long time to come as well as paying a percentage – usually three percent – of your funds as a handling fee. And, in the worst of worlds, you may max out your card completely. This is a way to become the Purser's office guest at debarkation when your credit card company says "No" to your onboard charges.
- Did you ever want to know why, when you hit a jackpot,

the first hundred or so coins spew out of the machine and the balance is paid by the staff? It's to keep a stash of coins in the machine for the next victims. Casino management wishes it could be different; winners who've just been handed the big bucks tend to leave the casino rather than playing on.

Whatever your gambling pleasure, get ready to hear the *cha-ching* of slot machines as soon as your ship clears U.S. coastal waters or leaves a foreign port. Chips ahoy !!!

90

CHAPTER EIGHT

SAIL BAG

This is the place where everything that didn't fit anywhere else ended up. At the end.

Deviant Behavior

Don't worry, you won't get arrested for this. The air travel provided by cruise lines is usually bargain-level and you may be scheduled to arrive or leave a port hours before or after the ship allows you to bark, whether em- or de-. Killing time during those hours is, at the very least, a drag.

For a nominal fee, usually around $50 per person, you can change the cruise line's air arrangements to flights that are more agreeable. But don't cut it too close.

Take the time to see if deviating or booking your own air to the departure port will save money or aggravation and figure out what it's worth to you. Often, if you make your own airline arrangements, you will be able to afford a pre-cruise night in a pleasant hostelry, resting up and making sure your luggage – should it have gone astray – catches up with you before sailing.

If you do book your own air, especially for travel on the day of sailing, and you are delayed or your flight is cancelled, the ship just may leave port without you because your travel records won't be in the Official Computer. Also, make sure, certain, positive about arrangements to get from a pre-cruise hotel to the pier.

So, what about pre- and post-cruise hotels if they're part of the package?

Tough question. Usually, hotel rooms are not available for check-in until early- to mid-afternoon and management wants you out of them on the early-morning side. Pre-cruise, ask nicely about a late check-out and confirm your transportation to the pier. Post-cruise, go to the hotel, ask where they're storing carry-on bags until the rooms are ready, grab your guidebook, and go out on the town. Never waste an hour when you could be sightseeing or shopping. Everyone else will be standing around and complaining; you'll be having fun. Every hotel in the universe will hold your luggage for you on the way out of town. If you're departing from an interesting city, from San Juan to Singapore, make every minute count and take a late flight.

To Your Good Health ...

I'm scared of being seasick. What's the best remedy?

It's hard to prove a negative – many people swear by one potion or remedy or another because they've never suffered the tortures of *mal de mer*. If you have, it's an experience you don't want to repeat.

There are over-the-counter remedies such as Dramamine, Dramamine II, and Bonine. Dramamine II and Bonine promise that they're non-drowsy, but they can provide the sensitive with a sound afternoon nap. During heavy weather, the Purser's Office or the ship's medical staff will probably be handing out a generic medicine upon request.

"The Patch", worn behind one ear, uses the drug scopolamine. "Scope" was used in years past to dope up ladies in labor. It still hurt, they just didn't remember. If The Patch doesn't work, you'll remember.

"Sea Bands" are stretchy, bracelet-like devices that work on the principle of acupressure. They look strange with cocktail dresses.

The alternative remedy of choice is ginger capsules, available at your local health food store, or plain crystallized ginger from your local grocery store. Some people take along a couple of bags of gingersnap cookies.

None of these will do much good if you're already ill. At the first sign of seasickness, usually a non-specific, minor sinus-type headache, take your medicine and get yourself to a weather deck. The worst thing you can do is take to your bunk, contemplating the pitching and rolling of the ship as your stomach pitches and rolls in unison with it.

If your stomach goes a bit south, avail yourself of a time-tested remedy. Ask the bartender for a glass of club soda and his little bottle of Angostura Bitters. Shake the bitters lustily into the soda (about ten shakes), mix and consume. A slice of lime is allowed for the sporty.

If the absolute worst happens, guard against dehydration. Eating apples provides plenty of fluid and they tend to stay down better than plain liquids. Call room service for some saltine crackers and an apple or two.

Ships' doctors are prepared to give anti-nausea injections for extreme cases.

If you take a variety of medicines on a regular basis, bring a list along with you. It's important that a new medicine not conflict with your regular doses.

What's the best cabin location on a ship so I won't get seasick?

The least motion is amidships, as low as possible. Modern ships are equipped with massive stabilization systems so the motion of the ocean is, usually, imperceptible. But the best place is still in the open air.

What kind of medical services can I expect to find on my ship?

For the most part, limited. Ships' hospitals are prepared to deal with minor cuts, sprains, burns and simple broken bones. They can handle first-line aid for heart attacks, strokes, and more serious injuries, but the passenger will probably be hospitalized at the next port of call and flown home on an emergency basis.

There are no dentists on cruise ships, except as passengers. Taking a dental anesthetic along in case of a toothache is a good plan. If you lose a crown, stick it back on with toothpaste. Chew carefully.

This brings us to one word: insurance. The cost of a flight home after hospitalization could keep you cruising for the rest of your natural life. Purchase insurance either through your cruise line/travel agent or from an outside source. But don't leave home without it. The cost is minimal. The security level is maximal.

Sometimes I use a walker, other times I need a wheelchair. Can I go on a cruise?

Of course. And more and more cruise lines are adapting cabins for wheelchair passengers. There will be wheelchairs available aboard, but you can't take them off the ship. Bring your own, preferably a lightweight model. You must travel with someone sufficiently able-bodied to assist you in case of emergency.

Ask your travel agent for a cabin as close as possible to the elevator bank that will take you most of the places you'll want to go. Putting up with a little noise in the corridor is preferable to a l-o-n-g walk or wheel.

And it's best not to get your hopes up for going ashore when a tender is required from ship to shore.

OK, Doc. Anything else I should take along, health-wise?

Yes. Over-the-counter preparations for the lower GI tract in both "Go" and "No Go" types. You don't want to spend any part of your cruise hanging around in the head with that Montezuma guy. Many cruisers, particularly women, suffer from the opposite problem. It may be the rich food, not drinking as much water as usual, or just the unfamiliar surroundings. But Mrs. Montezuma, who specializes in that opposite effect, gets her revenge, too. The problem compounds – if you take a laxative, do you want to guess when it is going to hit?

The best defense is a good offense. Right after boarding, drink two or three glasses of water, eat an apple, and take a mild laxative just to get things back on schedule after a hectic travel day.

If you have extra special medical needs be sure to check with the cruise line before you book. On one cruise out of New York, the ship stopped dead in the water just outside the harbor for about an hour. One of the passengers was on kidney dialysis and learned too late that the ship's power supply was the wrong voltage for a portable dialysis machine. That passenger had to be airlifted off the ship before the cruise could continue to Bermuda. Riding a rescue basket up to a hovering Coast Guard helicopter is a lousy way to begin a vacation.

Is it really O.K. to drink the water?

The standards for potable (drinkable) water aboard ships are probably far more stringent than your local water company's. Bottled designer water is free on six-star ships, part of the cabin complement on mid-range ships (for a charge) and practically non-existent on some other lines. Bring your own bottled water with you and re-fill the bottle from the bathroom tap to take ashore.

You may want to squeeze a slice of lemon or lime into the drinking water. Over-processed water can taste a bit flat.

Strangely, if you don't drink enough water, you'll tend to retain water to take care of what you haven't had. Fingers and feet swell. A mild diuretic is a good addition to the medical bag. Failing that, eat three cucumbers. A pill is preferable. Use the cucumbers for puffy eyelids.

Anything else for the ladies?

Well, yes. If you're "of a certain age" and Mother Nature hasn't paid one of her regular visits for quite a while, be prepared. You really don't want to send your husband to the disco at midnight to ask a hard-partying young lady, "Excuse, me Miss, but you wouldn't happen to have ..."

Listen to Mother

Two things we've always heard, "Wash your hands before eating," and "An apple a day keeps the doctor away," are golden rules on cruise ships.

Apples are a great source of fiber and pectin to keep our personal infrastructures working properly.

Remember when I said to take note of the less-public (rest) rooms? Before sitting down to dinner, wash your hands. How many people before you put their hands on the grand staircases' polished railings or the elevator buttons?

Are there any precautions I should take while onboard?

Sure. Wash your hands frequently. Most cold and flu germs are spread by contact, not by breathing. With so many passengers on board, there is a good chance that some of them have a cold. As a precaution whenever you touch something that someone else may have touched, wash your hands before you get them near your mouth or eyes. This includes those polished brass rails that line the halls and stairways. After you arrive at the doors to the dining room, duck into the restroom and lather up before you eat.

What if I drink too much and feel rotten the next day?

It's happened to lots of us. Before going to bed, take two (aspirin, ibuprofen, etc.) and drink two huge glasses of water. If you've really overindulged, put a glass filled with ice cubes next to your bed. By the time you wake up thirsty, it will be cold water. Put two more of those pain-relievers next to the glass.

Good Manners Afloat

I'm a smoker and I don't like to offend non-smokers. Are there special rules for ships?

There are some non-smoking ships, but you probably won't be taking one. Usually, smoking is permitted on one side of the ship and not the other. Look for the ashtrays on deck and in most of the lounges except the Main Show lounge. Some six-star liners have a smoking area in the dining room, but most ships don't. You can always sneak out of the dining room between courses if you really must smoke.

For safety reasons, don't wander around holding a lighted cigarette and whatever you do, don't toss cigarettes overboard. They might end up on a lower deck.

Newer ships feature cigar bars but, for the most part, pipe and cigar smoking is kept to the weather decks. You might want to stock up on smoking materials before leaving port to make sure that you'll have your favorite brand in sufficient quantity.

Warning: *Don't count on hitting a duty-free shop. Some keep capricious hours and don't have a wide selection when they are open.*

I don't smoke – can't stand it. But what if someone I really want to talk with smokes?

Ask if the person wouldn't mind sitting in a no-smoking area for a chat. I credit my friend Stephanie with the best line I've ever heard. "I just quit smoking and I'm afraid if I'm anywhere near smoking I may have to kill someone and steal their cigarettes."

Is there a graceful way to disengage from someone I really don't want to spend time with? We were "adopted" by a person on our last cruise and I couldn't figure out what to do.

Short of being rude or tossing the person overboard, consider this to be a test of your social skills. I don't know anyone who would say "Yes" if asked, "Do you mind if I join you?" Of course you'll hate giving up your prized lounge chair but, "Oh, but I was just leaving," is about the best you can do. Never mind if you just got there. Be wary of open-ended questions from your less-than-favorite people. "What are you doing tonight?" is a good example. In response to a specific invitation – say, for cocktails – an absent spouse is useful. "I'll need to check with Hector to see if he's made any plans." Unfortunately, the adoptive type doesn't take hints unless they're wrapped around cinder blocks.

We're so lucky. We always are in a cabin next door to a couple who fight (or love) loud and long late at night. Or, worse, have a screaming child. By day, they're delightful people, but I like to sleep.

This is a touchy one. We were kept awake all night during a rough crossing of the Tasmin Sea by the folks next door. They kept slamming dresser drawers. In retaliation, I slammed a few back at them since I was awake anyway. I was mortified when I saw them coming out of their cabin the next morning – two delightful ladies I'd played bridge with several times. As I was working up to my best blush, one lady inquired, "It sounds like you were having the same trouble with those self-opening drawers that we were." Fortunately, the ship's carpentry staff solved that one.

In the case of loud or lusty adults, mention the problem to the Purser. The offenders won't know if it was you, the cabin steward, or the people on the other side when they are approached and asked to keep it down.

Also speak with the Purser about the crying child. You can't stop the child from crying, but there may be another cabin available. Failing that, purchase earplugs at your next port stop if you forgot to pack them.

Babies are one thing. But what about uncontrolled bratty children?

Even though I am a strong proponent of the concept that Camp Grandma is the best place for children when Mom and Dad are on a cruise, today's busy lives seem to dictate that the whole family vacations together. If the parents won't or don't control their spawn, *carpe diem*. Walk up to the child/children in your most authoritative manner and simply tell them that they are behaving badly and if they don't stop it, you are going to tell your good friend, the Captain. This usually works.

If the obnoxiousness continues, find the parents and tell them that you are *certain* they have *no idea* what Bolivar and

Hermione are up to, and if they *did* know they would be horrified. That almost always works.

Tot and Teen Talk

My children are, almost always, well-behaved. Will other passengers have a problem with kids around? Will I?

All mainstream cruise lines have a "Kiddie Gulag" with trained counselors to keep the offspring busy so Mom and Dad can have fun, at least part of the time. Many also provide babysitting services after-hours for a reasonable fee. Kids usually fall in love with the program and can't wait to get shed of the parental units in favor of kid-based activities.

Programs for teens, sometimes including a separate disco, may operate only during busy, school-vacation timespans.

If you are possessed of a youngish one, the sort that still wears diapers, do not, DO NOT do as we've seen done too often – change the child's icky nappies in a public room.

It's tough on kids to travel during an "off-season" when most other kids are in school. They won't have many playmates (or disco-mates) aboard and will, predictably, become bored.

Will all four of us really fit into one cabin?

If you're traveling with children young enough to need a babysitter, you're not going to have much choice unless Mom sleeps in one cabin with Gladys and Dad sleeps in another with Ralph. In the best of all possible worlds, you'd travel with an *au pair* in a separate cabin with the kids – if you could keep her out of the disco.

If you're traveling with older kids and intend to share a cabin, forget everything you're read so far about organizing your cabin. The most rattled cruisers we've ever seen were sharing a cabin with two daughters, 14 and 16. The girls' hair and makeup were always perfect; Mom looked like she'd spent the entire day in a wind tunnel. Dad was decidedly grumpy. Separate cabins are worth the expense. Get an inside for the kids. You take an outside. Over-tip the cabin steward.

Can we really let older kids "out" on their own?

You know your kids. Either you trust them or you don't. Temptations aboard ship aren't much different from those at home, but may be more intense. Enlightened cruise lines make sure that the kids' sail-and-spend cards indicate that they're not old enough to purchase alcohol. But that won't stop anyone who's "legal" from buying a drink or two and passing it along.

Give teens a stern lecture on the subject of illegal, mood- and mind-altering substances. Sting operations on cruise ships are becoming more common. Getting busted in a foreign port will not add to the cruise experience or do much for family harmony.

And, a special note for those parents with pretty daughters. There are some very handsome and exotic men on cruise ships. Enough said.

OMIGOSH! We've been invited to dine with "The Master". What do we do?

You probably found the invitation under your door or on your bed. It says *"R.S.V.P." Respondez* immediately. (You will probably say yes.) The most elegant way is to write a small note of acceptance on the ship's stationery and deliver it to the front desk, but a phone call to the number on the invitation works as well. If you must decline, do so even more quickly.

> *Mr. And Mrs. Hopkins (cabin 1053)*
> *are delighted to accept the*
> *Master's invitation for dinner*
> *this evening at eight-thirty*

DO NOT BE LATE. You'll be told where to gather, usually in a lounge. The Captain probably won't be there, especially on the first formal night because he's doing his thing in the show room. The Social Hostess or a staff officer will meet you, make sure you have an appropriate libation, and introduce you to the other favored few.

After drinks, you'll be led to the Captain's table, which is always in a prominent spot. Don't trip over your hem; the whole dining room is watching. There are always place cards, so don't worry about where to sit.

There will be plenty of wine, if you so choose. The worst *gaffe* you can commit is to ask for another cocktail.

The Captain leads the dinner chat, usually beginning by speaking to the lady on his right. When the first course arrives, the "table turns" and the Captain speaks to the lady on his left. The rest of the table follows the same pattern with each subsequent course. With an amiable group, everybody is talking to everyone else by dessert.

A ship's photographer will come around to take a photo that you'll treasure for the rest of your life. Usually, the photo will show up in your cabin, compliments of The Master.

Write a thank-you note.

But my husband didn't bring a tux. Can we still join the Captain?

Of course. So long as he did bring a dark suit or, at the very least, a jacket and a tie. Many ships have a rent-a-tux facility.

We met a lovely couple on our last cruise and exchanged addresses. They invited us to visit "any time" – now we find out we will be near them on an upcoming trip. What to do?

Unless you became wildly fast friends, do not assume that the invitation includes house room at their residence. A note (or e-mail) telling them that you'll be in the area on certain dates and would love to see them again is the appropriate opening volley. Tell them where you will be staying or ask for a rooming recommendation. You want to take them to dinner. Let them set the boundaries.

At the same time, be a little bit careful about shipboard romances on your end when you extend an invitation. The folks who were the life of the party on board may be quite different on dry land.

Belt and Suspenders

Here are a few questions that you'd never need to know the answers to unless you are caught up in an unexpected maelstrom of legalities and other uglinesses.

I'm about to get married and we're cruising for our honeymoon. What do I do about changing my name?

You can't change your name until your name is changed, unless you want to go through bizarre hassles. The most important thing is that your travel documents match the other identification you have. If your passport or other ID is in your maiden name, make sure your cruise ticket says "Susie Smith" – your old name – rather than "Susie Jones" – your new one.

Hold on. I don't ever intend to become "Susie Jones". What about that?

The one and only place where it's belt-and-suspenders essential to use your "married" name is on your passport. If you're in a third-world country and either you or your spouse falls ill, you will need some proof that you are, in fact, married and you're able to order or approve medical care for your partner. Apply for a new passport and use your maiden or professional name as your "middle" name so it will match your other identification papers.

All my own identification, including my far too many credit cards and my driver's license are in the name you'll see on the cover of this book. My passport has "Kane" as the middle identifier and my husband's surname, "Hopkins", as my surname.

Now it's confusing. Some countries only ask for a photo ID and a raised-seal birth certificate, not a passport. What if I don't have the same last name as I did when I was born?

This confuses me, too. The belt-and-suspenders approach is to take along a copy of your marriage certificate.

I want to take my children on a special trip. I've heard horror stories of single parents or parents traveling* sans *spouse but with kids having a hard time. What's up? And what if my daughter takes her best friend along?

Airlines and cruise lines don't want to be party to a kidnapping. I ran into this situation myself as I stood at the airline check-in counter with my offspring. To be belt-and-suspenders careful, take along a notarized statement from the kids' other parent(s) that they're permitted to travel with you. To be super careful, make sure flight numbers and identification of the ship are included in the document. As a practical matter, if you're taking a domestic airline to a U.S. port, you probably won't have any trouble.

Why do I need to provide an emergency phone number with my travel papers?

For emergencies. The most likely one is a ship arriving late at its destination port. The Purser's office gets on the phone and starts calling those emergency numbers. Unless you've made arrangements for hired transportation from the port, in which case it's up to the livery company to check your schedule, make sure there's an emergency number that belongs to the person who's supposed to be picking you up, not to somebody at the office. Most cruises "turn" on weekend days.

Stormy Weather

What about hurricanes?

Hurricanes tend to occur in the August - November time frame. A cruise in Hurricane Alley during these months always carries a risk. But the risk isn't that you'll be caught in one. The risk is that you might leave port a day early to get out of the way, you might skip a port entirely, or you might think you're going to Hamilton (Bermuda) and end up in Halifax (Nova Scotia).

Rest assured that the Captain and the decision-makers at the cruise line are not going to put their expensive ship and your precious well-being in harm's way. Also take comfort in the fact that the slowest cruise ship can easily outrun one of Mother Nature's temper tantrums.

It's also possible that a hurricane will make a visit to your destination before your cruise. If there's been significant damage, the cruise line will probably decide to skip the port entirely or substitute another.

We were on a cruise from San Diego to San Juan when a Pacific hurricane lashed Acapulco, our first scheduled port-of-call, on the very day we left San Diego. The Captain wisely decided to skip Mexico and added Puerto Caldera, Costa Rica. By the time we arrived, the cruise line had set up a full schedule of shore excursions. The only inconvenience was five at sea days before making our first port. Some passengers kissed the ground when we arrived.

Reach out and Touch Someone

Can I call home from the ship? Can I check with my office? What about faxes? Or the Internet?

Yes, Yes, Yes, Maybe. Be warned. Making a phone call or sending a fax is very expensive. Not long ago, traveling with a friend, I sent a one-page fax to my husband in which I professed to be having a miserable time. The cost? Over $30. Then I *was* miserable! You can save money by calling from port. That's what most of the crew members do.

With the advent of the new *Norwegian Sky* and the first Internet Café afloat, we're seeing the shipboard communications revolution. You'll also find Internet Cafés in many port cities.

You might be considering packing the old laptop to do some work while you are on vacation. Unless you want to spend all day in your cabin, take along an extra battery pack. Then you can take the laptop out on deck and work away without the need to be near an outlet and still have power to spare. Outside of your cabin, electrical outlets of the type needed by most computers are generally in short supply. To be really careful, don't depend upon the ship's current. Go battery all the way, with one charging while you use another.

What if someone needs to call me?

Check your travel documents when they arrive. There will be instructions on how to reach the ship either by telephone or fax.

Love Me Tender

I'm not even sure what a tender is, but the brochure for the cruise I'm taking says that we will tender to a private island. What does that mean?

Assuming you know what a private island is, it means that you are taken off the ship into a boat – usually one of the ship's lifeboats – and then taken ashore. A platform is rigged and you step – with the assistance of crew – from the platform to the tender and back again.

The reason for tendering is that the ship's keel (the deep part under water) is simply too deep to come into shore. NCL's *Norway* always tenders into St. Thomas port; the harbor simply isn't deep enough to accommodate her depth of keel.

That doesn't sound like too much fun. What happens if there are a lot of waves?

If there are a lot of waves, you won't be tendering. It's simply too dangerous. The Captain decides on tendering operations and, sometimes, private islands are skipped in favor of an at-sea day because of weather and the associated safety factors.

But BE CAREFUL. That leap from platform to tender or back again isn't for the lame, the halt, or the inebriated. Wear sensible shoes, preferably with stick-to-the-deck soles. If you're lugging a lot of parcels on the way back, stare down the crew assistants and hand them the parcels first before you leap lithely from the tender. You want both hands available for the helpful crew members to get you transferred safely.

When you're on the tender, SIT DOWN. Tenders are not usually the smoothest rides in the world. They're slow, they wallow, and, especially in the Caribbean, it can be hot inside and the sun can be brutal up-top. If you have any tendency toward seasickness, this is the time to hit the anti-nausea meds.

Mother Nature's Alarm Clock

If you absolutely must wake up early – transiting the Panama Canal or catching the tender to St. John on the way to St. Thomas come immediately to mind – set your alarm clock, leave a wakeup call, order room service coffee and open your cabin's heavy draperies before retiring. Morning sun is a much kinder, gentler way to awaken than being blasted by electronic blappings or another human being.

Good Morning America

Or whatever your final port will be. There's a good reason for leaving this part for last. It's not fun, and I didn't want to spoil your cruise through the pages of this book.

Last Tango in Paris – or Onboard

This is the night when you wish the cruise could go on forever — particularly because there are a lot of nasty details demanding your attention.

The Envelope, Please ...

As if by magic, a number of small envelopes appeared in your cabin in the afternoon. They usually have cunning messages such as, "For My Cabin Steward." Your duty is clear. Stuff them with cash. The ship's newspaper will generally include some guidelines. Check back to Chapter Three for advice on tipping.

Bad News on the Doorstep

Sometime in the late afternoon a nice computer printout of everything you've charged to your sail-and-spend card will show up under your door, on the foot of your bed, or displayed on your desk. This is a "pre-bill", giving you the opportunity to dispute any charges you think are incorrect. Give it a glance for glaring errors. This is not the moment to take spouse or offspring to task for what they did, indeed, spend. If you were charged for a shore excursion you didn't take, a sequined tuxedo rental, or drinks in a bar on a night you were watching TV in the cabin, make a fuss. Now. If you don't, your final bill will be under the door in the morning, already charged to your credit card.

Packrat

Rats. Packing. On your last night out, after enjoying the camaraderie of new friends for the last time, you must repack all those suitcases you so carefully packed a lifetime ago. And have them in the hall by, usually – EEK! – 1:00 AM.

Wise cruisers do the re-pack late in the afternoon, leaving only the last-minute carryon for the morning. With luck, the packed bags will slide under the bed, out of the way. Otherwise, stack the packed bags tidily in a corner of your cabin to be put out later.

Some people choose to wear their next-day travel clothes to dinner. Others don't. Whichever your choice, don't forget you must be clothed tomorrow. There are plenty of sea-going legends about the folks who ever so carefully packed their last-night outfits and set the bags outside the door.

Check to make sure that your cruiseline baggage tags are still attached to your luggage. With luck, all the luggage from a particular deck ends up in the same area with their identifying tags, making your collection process easier. Don't expect all of your luggage to be together.

It's a good idea to have some special identification method for your luggage. A strip of colorful tape, a wildly-colored luggage strap or pompoms work well.

Wake Up and Smell the Coffee

Except, on debarkation day, it probably won't be delivered by room service. And, after a week or so of living without a morning schedule, one is imposed. As in, "Out of your cabin by 8:00 AM". Check the ship's newspaper to see where breakfast is being served. Sometimes the main dining room doesn't offer a seated, order-from-the-menu breakfast and you're on your own to fight with everyone else at the buffet.

There's a lot to be said for a bootlegged banana or apple on The Last Morning.

Ladies and Gentlemen in Waiting

The Number One activity as you wait – and wait and wait– at your arrival port is for the ship to be cleared and for passengers' shipboard accounts to be cleared. If you hear announcements asking for the same passengers' names over and over it's for one of two reasons. First, a passenger's credit card company said, "No." Second, a foreign national didn't complete the proper immigration paperwork.

The deadbeat will probably get off the ship. The foreign national will be detained so you can get off.

The only weapons here are a good book, a bottle of water or can of soda, a piece of fruit and a cheery attitude. Don't murder your vacation with impatience and surliness at the end.

You may very well spend more time in lines than in transit. You line up to get off the ship. Line up to get your luggage. Other queues for Customs, boarding a bus to the airport, and check-in for your flight. You line up to get off your plane, claim your baggage and, if your destination port was foreign, form a line for U.S. Immigration and Customs. And you thought the midnight buffet line was tough!

First On, First Off

Not exactly. Boarding is usually a fairly leisurely process over a period of three or four hours. Fleeing the ship is much more intense. Debarkation cards with a number (or a letter, or a color) appear in your cabin on the night of The Last Supper. You'll be called to leave the ship in a pre-determined order, based on that card.

People with fast flight connections usually receive preference as do the handicapped and those in top cabins.

In the meantime, the public rooms are filled with "huddled masses." Do your best to be cheerful. And don't jam the passageways.

Home Port

Your front door probably never looked so good. The mail can wait. The unpacking surely can wait. The dog can stay at the kennel for another day. Or the kids with Grandma. And you really don't need to eat again, do you?

Think about those clean sheets in the bedroom, reach into the fridge and haul out the bottle of Champagne and the block of good cheese you stashed before departure, get the crackers from the pantry, put your feet up and start the first of a lifetime's reminisces.

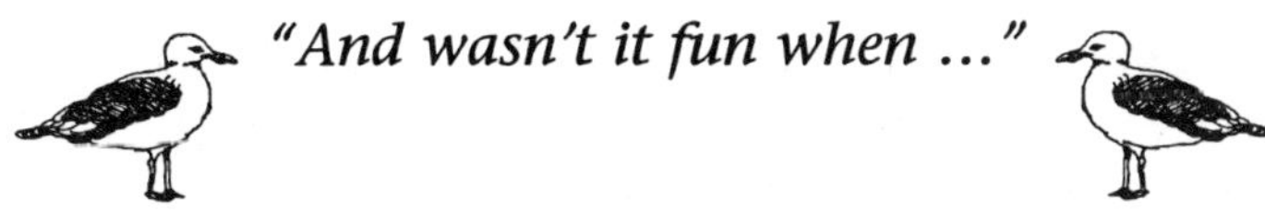

Welcome
Home